Pathways to Knowledge®
and Inquiry Learning

Information Literacy Series

Pathways to Knowledge® and Inquiry Learning

Marjorie L. Pappas

Ann E. Tepe

2002
LIBRARIES UNLIMITED
Teacher Ideas Press
A Division of Greenwood Publishing Group, Inc.
Greenwood Village, Colorado

This book is dedicated to our families with love and appreciation. We also dedicate this to our long-time friendship and to future projects.

LIBRARIES UNLIMITED
Teacher Ideas Press
A Division of Greenwood Publishing Group, Inc.
7730 East Belleview Avenue, Suite A200
Greenwood Village, CO 80111
1-800-225-5800
www.lu.com

Library of Congress Cataloging-in-Publication Data

Pappas, Marjorie, 1938-
   Pathways to knowledge and inquiry learning / Marjorie L. Pappas, Ann E. Tepe.
      p. cm. -- (Information literacy series)
   Includes bibliographical references and index.
      ISBN 1-56308-843-6 (pbk.)
      1. Questioning. 2. Inquiry (Theory of knowledge) 3. Information retrieval--Study and teaching. I. Tepe, Ann E., 1946- II. Title. III. Series.

LB1027.44 .P37 2002
370.15'23--dc21
                                                                              2001050747

Contents

Acknowledgments

We thank the following individuals for their help and suggestions: Gayle Geitgey, Barbara Greenlief, Cynthia Kiefer, and Carol Webb. We also thank Edward Roark for his photography and the library media specialists of Jessamine County (Kentucky) for providing us opportunities to show students pursuing inquiry in libraries.

Introduction

Young children are extremely curious, with an insatiable appetite for questioning everyone. "Mommy, why is that bee on my flower?" "Where does snow come from?" "Why does Uncle George have hair on his face?" Children are in a perpetual state of discovery or inquiry. When they are introduced to picture books they love listening to stories being read and raise many questions. Sometimes they will return to the same question over and over, obviously intrigued with a particular concept. Young children seem instinctively able to practice inquiry. They question and question. Their questions, often put to adults in their world, are a way of gathering information. They continue to question until they lose interest or construct a personal understanding of the concept that aroused their curiosity.

In formal schooling the concept of inquiry has been a part of the science curriculum in the form of scientific inquiry. The social sciences have also used the idea of inquiry in relation to disciplines such as history (historical inquiry) and sociology. Archeologists have long pursued a form of inquiry in their study of ancient worlds. Today inquiry has begun to permeate all areas of the curriculum. Teachers are using the idea of inquiry to foster student-centered learning and critical thinking.

One day a group of fourth-grade students at Rosenwald–Dunbar Elementary School (RDES) in Nicholasville, Kentucky, came to school with lots of questions and concerns about a coal company's plans for removing the top of Black Mountain, Kentucky's highest peak. Mining companies had begun using mountaintop removal as one of the methods of coal mining. Sandy Adams, a fourth-grade teacher, facilitated the discussion that day, and the entire class became engaged in the issue. Students were excited, raised many questions, and wanted to learn more about mountaintop removal. So, Adams rewrote her upcoming unit plans using mountaintop removal as the content to correlate with required state standards.

Barbara Greenlief, library media specialist (LMS) at RDES, began working collaboratively with Adams and her students as they gathered information from the library media center, local and state offices, local experts, and the World Wide Web. Students raised money and traveled to Harlan County, where Black Mountain is located, to talk directly with people who would be affected by the removal of Black Mountain's top. Students testified at legislative hearings, held rallies to raise public awareness of the problem, wrote proposals, and interacted with local journalists. Students at RDES began working collaboratively with students from a high school in Harlan County in a campaign to stop the mountaintop removal process.

These students generated so much public attention about the issue that local and national news services began to pick up the story. The spotlight was then focused on Kentucky lawmakers, who were trying to resolve the issue. In the spring, students learned that their efforts had been successful. A legislative committee worked out a compromise with the mining company, and Black Mountain was saved (S. Adams and B. Greenlief, personal communication, May 1999). These students moved from an initial stage of curiosity into a full-blown inquiry-driven investigation of a real-world problem. This was not an isolated experience. Students learn to use inquiry from the beginning of their time at RDES.

The notion of process as opposed to content is an important part of constructivism, and process is taking a more prominent place in standards and curriculum today. (Chapter 2 covers constructivism.) English/language arts teachers teach students to write using the writing process. Process has a long history among scientists, who regularly apply the scientific method as they pursue their research. Carol Kuhlthau connected process with the broader realm of information seeking in her research studies involving high school students who were gathering information for research papers (Kuhlthau, 1985). Many information process models evolved from that research, including *The Big6*™ (Eisenberg and Berkowitz, 1990, 1999), *Taxonomy of Thoughtful Research* (Stripling and Pitts, 1988), *The Research Cycle* (see McKenzie, 2000), *Flip IT!* (Yucht, 1997) and *Pathways to Knowledge*® (Pappas and Tepe, 1997). Process in this context reflects stages or steps that information seekers follow as they identify their information need, then gather, evaluate, organize, and use information. (See the Pathways model in Appendix A.)

We focus on inquiry learning and the Pathways model in this book. Our goal is to show you practical ideas for applying both Pathways and inquiry to your curriculum and instructional practices. We tend to be global learners, so we set the stage by showing you how Pathways fits into the big picture of education. Switzer and Callahan (2000) developed the *Technology As a Facilitator of Quality Education* model (INTIME) shown in Figure I.1 as a framework for a three-year Catalyst Grant to the University of Northern Iowa's College of Education.

The purpose of INTIME is to provide the necessary resources for methods faculty to revise their courses, model technology integration, and require preservice teachers to integrate technology, along with components of quality education, in their lessons and units. A consortium of five participating Renaissance Group universities has come together in this project to create new learning resources and implement new standards for technology integration in preservice teacher education.

INTIME is a student-centered model. Switzer and Callahan have used a circle graphic to show how Principles of Learning, Information Processing, Content Standards, and the Tenets of Democracy relate to students in the larger, more global view. The Pathways to Knowledge stages have been incorporated in Figure I.1 to represent Information Processing.

Figure I.1. Technology As Facilitator of Quality Education Model.
Source: **Switzer and Callahan (2000).**

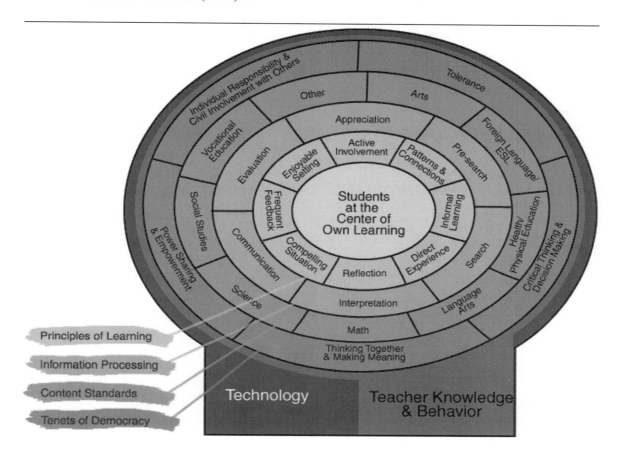

This book is organized into five chapters and includes a variety of scenarios, which we hope will help you understand what inquiry learning and Pathways might look like in practice. Some of the scenarios have accompanying unit planning guides in the appendixes. Our goal is to give you ideas for thematic units and an authentic approach to unit design, but we understand that you will need to change and adjust these units to suit your specific needs. Some of the units are more teacher directed, while others show examples of student choice. *(Note: All scenarios, including names and locations, are fictitious. Any similarity to real persons, places, or situations is unintended.)*

OVERVIEW

Chapter 1 provides an in-depth focus on the Pathways to Knowledge model. Short scenarios show how stages and strategies might be applied with students in various thematic units.

Chapter 2 is about inquiry learning, with some background information about constructivism and contemporary curriculum design.

Chapter 3 covers background information on information literacy and collaboration, then shows a curriculum design process, including an example of a unit planning guide. Library media specialists and teachers often struggle with where to begin teaching students about the Pathways model and how to keep track of those strategies that students have experience using. A blank version of the Pathways model appears in Appendix A as Figure A.3 to use for recording the strategies used (formally taught) by students.

Chapter 4 explores the tools of technology and how students might use these as they apply the stages of Pathways to their own information-seeking process.

Chapter 5 shows how library media specialists, teachers, and administrators might use a change process to implement inquiry learning and Pathways into the curriculum.

TERMINOLOGY: WEB ADDRESSES

We struggled a bit about the words to use for teachers and library media specialists. We understand that there are many types of teachers in a school (e.g., classroom teachers, special teachers, library media specialists). Sometimes a sentence was less wordy when we used *teacher,* and in that context we were referring to all types of teachers in a school, including library media specialists.

Another dilemma we faced was the use of *learner* or *student.* You will find these used interchangeably in the book. *Learner* tends to be our preference, but sometimes the use of that word in combination with *learning* was awkward, so *student* was used. In chapters 1 and 4, in which we focus on the actual search process, we found ourselves using *information seeker* or *searcher.* We did this because anyone—adult or child—might be applying an information process like Pathways, so it seemed inappropriate to limit the focus to only students in a school setting. We used *information seeker* and *searcher* interchangeably.

In most cases, Web addresses can be found in a separate Web Resources list at the end of each chapter. Web addresses can be very long and cumbersome and interrupt the flow of ideas within the text itself. However, in a limited number of situations, the Web address is within the text.

REFERENCES

Note: All Web addresses accessed December 21, 2001.

Eisenberg, M. B., and R. E. Berkowitz. (1990). *Information problem-solving: The Big Six skills approach to library and information skills instruction.* Norwood, NJ: Ablex.

Eisenberg, M. B., and R. E. Berkowitz. (1999). *Teaching information & technology skills: The Big6™ in elementary schools.* Worthington, OH: Linworth.

Kuhlthau, C. C. (1985). *Teaching the library research process.* West Nyack, NY: The Center for Applied Research in Education.

McKenzie, J. (2000). *Beyond technology: Questioning, research and the information literate school.* Bellingham, WA: FNO Press.

Pappas, M. L., and A. E. Tepe. (1997). *Pathways to Knowledge®*. McHenry, IL: Follett Software. Available: http://www.pathwaysmodel.com.

Stripling, B. K., and J. M. Pitts. (1988). Taxonomy of thoughtful research. In *Brainstorms and Blueprints: Teaching library research as a thinking process.* Englewood, CO: Libraries Unlimited.

Switzer, T. J., and W. P. Callahan. (2000). *Technology as a facilitator of quality of education: A Model.* [Online] Available: http://www.intime.uni.edu/model/modelarticle.html.

Yucht, A. H. (1997). *FLIP IT! An information skills strategy for student researchers.* Worthington, OH: Linworth.

1

Pathways
to Knowledge®

Pathways to Knowledge® is a process model that can be used by anyone who wants to find, use, and evaluate information. In this chapter we describe the Pathways model and show how students in various learning scenarios might use it.

The Pathways model has been developed in two formats. One is a graphic version that shows the stages and strategies of the model laid out in curved bands. The graphic was designed purposely to reflect the nonlinear aspect of the searching process. The other version of the model is the Extended Text Version, which presents the stages and strategies in descriptive form and includes additional details about each stage. Both versions of the Pathways model are in Appendix A.

OVERVIEW OF THE PATHWAYS MODEL

The stages of the Pathways model appear across the top of the graphic version (see Figure A.1 in Appendix A). The strategies are arranged in bands under each stage and are included to provide the information seeker with a wide variety of options. Those seeking information should understand that, typically, only a few of these strategies will be used in any specific research project or to fulfill any information need. The model is a holistic process, so we explain it here in a holistic manner before exploring specific stages and strategies.

Pathways Is a Nonlinear Process

The Pathways model has been designed to show that the information-seeking process is nonlinear. Professional information specialists (e.g., librarians) often pursue different pathways to finding and using information. This is partially related to differing learning styles and the nature of the information need. It seems appropriate to teach students that a nonlinear approach is not only accepted but is the norm. A serious effort was made to design the Pathways model so that the nonlinear nature of the process would be evident in the graphic version. The layout of the curved bands and the arrows that suggest a back-and-forth progression are visual clues of a nonlinear progression.

Stages of the Pathways Model

The Pathways model is composed of six stages: Appreciation, Presearch, Search, Interpretation, Communication, and Evaluation. The Appreciation and Evaluation stages transcend all the others. Appreciation is not necessarily a stage that must occur at the beginning of information seeking but rather continues throughout the process. Evaluation must occur within each stage and not just at the end of the process.

Function Statements

Function statements describe the primary actions information seekers will pursue within each stage. On the graphic version of the model there is **bold text** that appears in the first band of each section, with the exception of Appreciation. These are function statements. The model includes the following function statements:

Appreciation—No function statement

Presearch—Establishing my focus

Search—Planning and implementing my search strategy

Interpretation—Assessing usefulness of my information; reflecting to develop my personal meaning

Communication—Constructing and presenting my new knowledge

Evaluation—Thinking about my process and product

The function statements are presented in the first person to personalize each stage for the information seeker.

Pathways Strategies

The Pathways model includes general and specific strategies. The general strategies are those statements that appear in the circles beginning with Presearch. These were developed to give the information seeker a broader view of the specific strategies within each stage. The general strategies are listed in Table 1.1.

As it is shown in this arrangement, an information seeker might decide that Pathways is a linear process. However, keep in mind that the research process can begin with a variety of general strategies. For example, Sara wants to purchase a new computer. Her information need is to locate information about the price of computers, components, and rating of models so that she can make an informed decision. She knows that the latest issues of the computing magazines have articles that describe and rate all the new computer models. She starts her search with the general strategy *Select information resources and tools*.

Table 1.1 Pathways Stages and Strategies

Pathways Stage	Pathways General Strategies
Appreciation	No general strategy
Presearch	Develop an overview Explore relationships
Search	Identify information providers Select information resources Seek relevant information
Interpretation	Interpret information
Communication	Apply information Share new knowledge
Evaluation	Evaluate process and product

As Sara peruses several computing magazines, she realizes there are so many options and features that she must first decide which of these she wants to have in her computer. She needs to establish a more narrow focus for her search, which causes her to apply a Presearch strategy. Sara began her information seeking in the Search stage, which is where many information seekers often begin, but then went to Presearch. Her next step will be back to Search. This process of moving around in the stages of Pathways reflects a nonlinear path through the model.

Within each general strategy there are specific strategies. These strategies represent a range of options available to information seekers, who must select those strategies that are most appropriate for their specific information need or research project. Many strategies are shown on the graphic version of the Pathways model.

Extended Text Version

The graphic version has limitations due to space. The Extended Text Version, on the other hand, contains a more complete list of strategies. The Extended Text Version is a linear representation of the graphic Pathways model and includes a descriptive paragraph about each stage. The function statements and general strategies are included with each stage in a similar manner to the graphic version but often include additional specific strategies. Many of the specific strategies were developed in language that can be used in curriculum documents as part of outcome or benchmark statements.

The following sections explore each stage of the model in depth.

APPRECIATION

SCENARIO 1.1

Mrs. Rogers's seventh-grade art class is creating murals that depict daily life in Native American villages. The students are also studying Native Americans in their social studies class with another teacher, Mr. James. Mrs. Rogers began this art project by showing students a sampling of mural reproductions from her personal collection. She asked them to talk about how the murals were different and how each mural represented various cultures. Several students remembered seeing murals when they were traveling in the western United States. Their discussion led them to be curious about the artists who painted murals and the different techniques each of them used. The students decided they needed more information about styles and techniques related to murals. They also wanted to find more examples, specifically those that might have come from Native American cultures.

They decided to assign different information resources or providers to small groups in the class. One group checked out the resources in their school library, where the library media specialist helped them use the catalog and periodical databases. Another visited a local museum that had a Native American art exhibit. Another group visited the library media center and did some searching on the Web. They found the NativeWeb site to be very helpful. Several days later they shared their new information. They were very excited about all the different examples of murals they were able to find. After some discussion, the students decided that if they were going to create authentic murals, they needed more information about Native American tribes that actually created murals. So they returned to gathering information.

The Pathways model provides the following description of the Appreciation stage:

> *Individuals appreciate literature, the arts, nature and information in the world around them through varied and multiple formats, including stories, film, paintings, natural settings, music, books, periodicals, the Web, video, etc. Appreciation often fosters curiosity and imagination, which can be a prelude to a discovery phase in an information seeking activity. As learners proceed through the stages of information seeking their appreciation grows and matures throughout the process.*

Students in Mrs. Rogers's class began by viewing pictures of murals. Their subsequent discussion caused them to be curious about different types of murals and the techniques used to create these pictures. Their curiosity led them to gather information using search strategies, and they evaluated this information in their class discussion. Their evaluation created an enjoyment of this art form that they verbalized in their discussion. After some analysis of the information, they realized that they needed to search for more information.

In Scenario 1.1, students began their research process by viewing pictures, an Appreciation strategy, but they used other stages of the Pathways model as they pursued their research project. In previous research assignments, students had begun with a research topic, using Presearch and Search strategies to gather information. At various times in their process they may come across a story, picture, video, or artistic piece, or even visit a local park. Each of these provides them with information but also opportunities to apply Appreciation strategies such as enjoying, listening, reading, or viewing.

Appreciation is an important element of the research process, and all learners should be aware of when they are using this stage. The importance of Appreciation is underscored in the *Information Literacy Standards for Student Learning* (AASL and AECT, 1998). Standard five states: "The student who is an independent learner is information literate and appreciates literature and other creative expressions of information." (p. 26).

PRESEARCH

SCENARIO 1.2

Susan and Tara have begun to explore animal habitats. Their teacher, Mr. Simms, talked with the class about the places where animals live and why they choose those places. The students in their class brainstormed and made a web about the places where animals live, but the web was limited in scope. They knew that the pond, just beyond the playground, and the forest in the park were habitats but could not name any others. Mr. Simms suggested they might go to the library media center to gather some general information about habitats.

Susan found a great article in the science encyclopedia that had many pictures showing animal habitats. She learned that deserts, marshes, and swamps can also be habitats. Susan had never heard about a marsh before, so she located some general information in the encyclopedia. Miss Lewis, the library media specialist, suggested the students might try looking in the electronic encyclopedia using the subject tree. Both Susan and Tara were amazed at how many habitats that search produced. "If you want specific information on any of those habitats listed in the hierarchical list, you will need to search for each animal and its habitat," Miss Lewis told them.

When the students returned to their classroom, Mr. Simms asked them to share their new information, which he added to the web they had developed earlier. "Now," Mr. Simms said, "You have a web that shows many of the habitats that animals use. How might we discover which of these habitats are located around where we live?"

The function of the Presearch stage is to establish a focus for the research project or information need. In this stage information seekers can develop an overview of their topic and explore any relationships between this topic and other related ideas or concepts. The Pathways model provides the following description of the Presearch stage:

> *The Presearch stage enables searchers to make a connection between their topic and prior knowledge. They may begin by brainstorming a web or questions that focus on what they know about their topic and what they want to know. This process may require them to engage in exploratory searching through general sources to develop a broad overview of their topic and explore the relationships among subtopics. Presearch provides searchers with strategies to narrow their focus and develop specific questions or define information needs.*

Presearch is one of the most important parts of the research process, yet it is one of the most underused. Often, when students begin a research project, their topic is either too broad or too narrow. They need to use Presearch strategies like building background information, exploring general sources of information, or brainstorming ideas and information about their topic, which can help them develop a sense of the big picture and see some of the relationships between their topics or ideas.

In Scenario 1.2, Tara and Susan knew about some animal habitats but needed more information to see the broad picture of habitats. The subject tree of the electronic encyclopedia provided them with a list of many animal habitats with links to articles that would give them some general background information on each habitat and the animals that live in it.

Often students are trying to find information about a topic that has absolutely no meaning to them. They cannot relate the topic to any prior experience or learning opportunity. Cognitive psychologists tell us that learning takes place as learners make connections between their existing mental schema and the new information just acquired. When that link is not apparent, students can become frustrated. Their research process lacks focus and becomes very inefficient. Students must recognize when this situation has occurred and apply appropriate strategies to help fill that gap between existing knowledge in their schema and a new research topic. One of the best strategies is to look in a general resource like an encyclopedia. A marsh habitat was a new idea to Sara, but she found some general information in the science encyclopedia. Exploring general sources like an encyclopedia or an almanac can be a very useful strategy at this point in the research process. The encyclopedia may only provide learners with a short summary of their topic, but that might be enough to relate the topic to a past memory or experience.

Brainstorming can also be a useful strategy and might be pursued either in a group or individually. As students brainstorm they can create a web (e.g., see Figure 1.1) or develop a list of statements and/or questions about their topic. For example, a KWL chart allows them to identify what they **K**now, what they **W**ant to know, and what they **L**earned about a topic.

Figure 1.1. Animal Habitat Web.

Animal Habitat Web

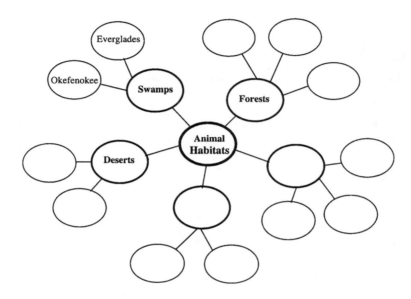

Throughout this Presearch stage students should be developing questions about their topic that focus on what they want to know or are related to the initial essential question asked by their teacher. Before they leave this stage, students should develop a specific research question or identify an information need. That provides them with a focus for the search process.

SEARCH

SCENARIO 1.3

Mrs. Hunter's high school health class is studying the effects of alcohol and smoking, particularly on young people. Mrs. Hunter asked the class how the effects of smoking and alcohol abuse influenced the lives of people. These students have been using the Pathways model throughout the year, so they know the stages and strategies fairly well. They began their project by brainstorming a list of questions that might be related to the broad question asked by their teacher. Then they divided their list of questions into related subtopics and formed small groups to gather information. Several students wanted to interview people from a local Alcoholics Anonymous group and the health department.

The students met with the library media specialist to talk about information providers who might have information about their subtopic. They decided that both the public library and the university library might be helpful. Mr. Foster, the school library media specialist, reviewed the use of SIRS Researcher. He also suggested that they might find some useful information by using both Yahoo and Google. Each group had developed a research question, and they used a keyword graphic organizer given to them by Mr. Foster to plan specific search strategies. Several students found books in the collection by using the electronic catalog; others used databases to find articles in magazines. One student found a collection of fact sheets on addictions on a Web site titled the *Web of Addictions*. Other students called the health department and set up an interview with a social worker. As they began to gather information, students used the T chart given them by Mr. Foster to gather information about their topic on one side of the page and their thoughts and reactions on the other side. As students compared their information in small groups, they discovered that they had some conflicting information about the results of alcoholism. Mr. Foster suggested that they needed to find at least one other source to validate their information.

The function of the Search stage is to plan and implement a search strategy. The Pathways model provides the following description of the Search stage:

> *During the Search stage, searchers identify appropriate information providers, resources and tools, then plan and implement a search strategy to find information relevant to their research question or information need. Searchers are open to using print and electronic tools and resources, cooperative searching and interaction with experts.*

This stage is probably the one element of the process that teachers, library media specialists, and students have emphasized the most. However, technology has greatly changed the search process, and information seekers who do not understand a search process and specific strategies will soon learn that technology, specifically the World Wide Web, can be very frustrating.

Tools, Resources, and Information Providers

Information and resources are available today in many locations beyond the walls of the school classroom and library media center. The learning environment is open, with an array of information providers. It is important for students to consider all potential information providers as they develop a plan for finding information related to their research question or information need. Classroom teachers and library media specialists must assist students in this process. One way to help might be to hold a brainstorming session with students about potential information providers. This list could include local libraries (e.g., academic, public, private), nature centers, historical sites, planetariums, zoos, museums, cable television, and community businesses and industry. Some examples are provided on the graphic version of the Pathways model, but classroom teachers and library media specialists should understand that this is only a representative list. Each local area will have unique information providers that should be considered when students are working on a research project.

In Scenario 1.3 the students in Mrs. Hunter's class discussed possible information providers and identified the local public and academic libraries, the local Alcoholics Anonymous Association, and the health department as potential information providers. These are high school students, so they might make those connections without any facilitation on the part of the classroom teacher or library media specialist. Classroom teachers who have younger students might want to make some initial contacts with these information providers before sending students out to gather information. For example, doctors or social workers in the community might be able to provide some valuable insights into the alcohol abuse problem, but a call from the teacher beforehand might pave a smoother route to an interview.

As students continue to develop a plan for finding information relative to their research question, they also must consider appropriate information tools and resources. The possibilities for resources seem almost limitless in this world of information access at both the local and global level. However, some resources will be more useful or more available than others. Efficiency becomes an important element in this information-seeking process.

Students should begin with information tools because these tools enable access to information. An information tool might be a catalog (print or electronic), an index, a bibliography, a search engine, a subject tree, or a database. At this point, students are confronted with the issue of which information tool(s) to select. Important criteria to consider are:

♦ *Time frame*. Is the topic current or historical? Information on current topics will be more readily available in periodicals rather than in books. By the time a book is published, the information is typically more than a year old. Historical information can be found in periodicals but more likely will be available in books. Historical information on the Web is growing through the sites that store the information in primary source documents such as old newspapers, diaries, and maps. Current information can be found by using periodical indexes or databases and Web search engines and subject trees.

♦ *Scope and depth*. Does the research question require a broad scope or narrow, shallow or deep level of information? Information that is broad in scope and with depth about the topic will more likely be found in a library's book collection. To locate this information, students should use the catalog. Some Web sites will also provide information that is rich and broad in scope. To locate this information, students should use Web indexes, subject trees, and search engines. Information that is shallow or narrow is typically located in general reference resources (e.g., encyclopedias, almanacs, atlases).

♦ *Location*. Is the topic related to local, state, national, or international issues? Local and state information is typically more difficult to find than national or international information because local information tools are not as readily available. Locally produced bibliographies, indexes, or databases would be useful tools. On a broader scale, using catalogs, indexes, and databases or Web-based indexes, subject trees, and search engines can help locate national and international information.

The students in Mrs. Hunter's class (Scenario 1.3) used both the catalog and periodical databases to find resources about alcohol abuse. *SIRS Researcher* is a full-text database, so the information tool (i.e., the database) and resources are held within the same software.

Information resources include books, magazines, video, film, audiotapes or discs, radio, people, artifacts, Web-based resources, CD-ROMs, multimedia, maps, newspapers, and pictures. Many students have a tendency to begin their search with the Web, but sometimes the best information and the most efficient route to that information are through the use of a book found in the library media center.

Once resources have been located, students need strategies to appropriately use the resources. Students learn to use books at a young age. They learn that books are organized in a linear manner, with pages numbered consecutively and text read in a left-to-right, top-to-bottom sequence. They also learn that a book has a table of contents and an index, tools to help them locate information efficiently in the book. The index is organized in alphabetical order, another linear sequence. Electronic information is organized in a nonlinear manner using hyperlinks (buttons, hot spots, etc.) that make connections from one page or item of information to another. This nonlinear aspect requires different skills for searching. Regardless of the format, linear or nonlinear, it is important for students to be able to use information resources appropriately.

Another type of information resource is people, including a conversation with parents or grandparents, professional people, fire and safety personnel, students in other places, or experts who communicate through the Web. For example, students in Mrs. Hunter's class interviewed a social worker in the health department of their town. Interviewing is another strategy for effectively using an information resource and requires prior planning and well-developed questions.

Developing Search Strategies for
Print and Electronic Resources

People who search for information in the print environment (e.g., books, magazines) use strategies that they have developed over time. For example, many nonfiction books have both a table of contents and an index. Either of those tools is a more efficient way to find specific information within the resource than simply reading through the text from beginning to end. If there are strategies for locating information in print resources, then it is logical that there should be strategies for locating information in the electronic environment. Typically, what information seekers know initially are those strategies used with print resources. That represents their prior knowledge. The search strategies on the Pathways model begin with those strategies, using the same common language, then extend beyond that to strategies that apply only to electronic resources.

The Pathways model includes four specific search strategies for finding information within print and electronic resources: Explore search, Browse search, Hierarchical search, and Analytical search.

Explore Search

An Explore search is looking, "surfing," and hyperlinking with a general topic. In the print environment, an information seeker might pursue an Explore search by using the table of contents, casually thumbing through records in a catalog with only a general topic in mind, or using chapter headings and subheadings in a book. This method of Explore searching tends to follow a more linear pathway, whereas in the electronic environment the pathway is nonlinear. For example, an information seeker might hyperlink from one Web page or site to another or from one article to another in a CD-ROM resource.

Whether in the print or electronic environment, there is a useful purpose to applying an Explore search for finding information. Typically, information seekers who engage in an Explore search lack focus regarding their research topic. They are more casually interested in the information they might find. Sometimes this is similar to looking through a coffee table book: It's just fun to look at the pictures and enjoy the scenery. This takes on the guise of appreciation, which relates back to the Appreciation stage of the Pathways model. Many people enjoy hyperlinking through Web sites in this manner, indulging their curiosity, and discovering new ideas. Sometimes Explore searching enables information seekers to build background information or make connections to prior knowledge, which are strategies related to Presearch. Sometimes it stimulates redirection of the search topic.

Browse Search

A Browse search is examining a list or index by topic. In the print environment, indexes and bibliographies are fairly common information tools. Both of these information tools are organized in an alphabetical sequence, which is a linear organization of information. To locate information using a print index, an information seeker would look for the subject or word related to the research topic within the alphabetical sequence of words, then use the accompanying page number(s), volume number, or issue number to find the information in book text, specific volume, or magazine. For example, a student in Mrs. Hunter's class might find information on alcohol abuse in several magazines by looking under that topic in the *Readers' Guide to Periodical Literature* (H. W. Wilson). When the subject is found, there might be a list of entries, and each of these entries typically will include the title of the article, author, volume, issue, and page number, which becomes the location information.

The electronic environment also includes indexes, which are usually features in specific resources or separate information tools on the Web. Electronic indexes are lists of titles, subjects, or both arranged in an alphabetical or numerical sequence. Locating information by using an electronic index requires the information seeker to key in a word or title in a search box or select the appropriate letter from the alphabet, then select a title from the resulting list that follows in the next window or screen. As a feature in an electronic resource, electronic indexing software searches only through the alphabetical list, not through the full text of the resource.

For example, one of Mrs. Hunter's students might have started the information-seeking process about alcohol abuse by looking in the *Grolier's Multimedia Encyclopedia* (Grolier), which has a feature called Browse, to locate some background information (Presearch strategy). This Browse feature is an alphabetical list of article titles that appear in the encyclopedia. A portion of this list is visible in a window on the screen, and the list changes in relation to the topics that are keyed into the search box positioned above the title list window. This feature does not search the full text of the encyclopedia but only the title list.

Hierarchical Search

A Hierarchical search is examining a body of knowledge from a broad concept to a specific topic. There are very few examples of print resources that reflect a hierarchical structure or organization of information. Some science books have sections that show classifications of scientific elements, and the print version of the ERIC Thesaurus is organized in a hierarchical manner. The electronic environment includes a growing number of tools and resources with a hierarchical feature for locating information. Many of these hierarchical features are called *subject trees*, or *directories*. On the Web, examples of directories are *Yahoo*, *Yahooligans*, and *Look Smart*.

To locate information using a Hierarchical search strategy, the information seeker first selects a topic from a list of disciplines or broad subject areas. If the information seeker cannot make that first connection, then a Hierarchical search strategy will not work for her. When that first selection is made, a new screen or window opens, showing another list of more specific topics. This process continues until a list of article titles appears and the information seeker can hyperlink from the article title to the full text of the article. Typically, this process would include a minimum of three window changes.

Several students in Mrs. Hunter's class searched *Yahoo*, a directory, for information on alcohol abuse. On the *Yahoo* start-up page they selected *Health* from the list of general subjects. As new windows appeared, they selected *drugs*, then *substance abuse*, and *alcoholism* from subsequent subject lists that appeared in windows. The last topic selection finally opened a list of articles about alcohol abuse.

Analytical Search

An Analytical search is electronically searching specified or full text using key-word, Boolean, concept searching, and so forth. Analytical search features are feasible only in the electronic environment. Searching through the full text of a print resource and examining the text for a topic is certainly possible, but this process would be time-consuming and not very efficient. Searching through full text for two subjects that are related in a print resource would be almost impossible. Analytical searching features are what make electronic resources so powerful in terms of locating information, especially when the information seeker is trying to find words or phrases that are related in some way.

Analytical searching is represented on the Web and in CD-ROM resources in a tool called a *search engine*. A search engine is software that looks for specified words or phrases in databases and/or the full text of resources. Search engine software can be part of an electronic resource such as an encyclopedia, periodical database, or full text magazines. For example, *Encarta Encyclopedia* is a full text resource located on CD-ROMs and on the Web. Both versions include a search engine to help information seekers find specific information. Search engines are also stand-alone tools on the Web that enable information seekers to look for specific information located on Web sites. For example, *Google*, *Excite*, and *Alta Vista* are search engines on the Web.

Many electronic resources have features that allow an information seeker to do both a simple and a complex search. A simple search requires an information seeker to key in one word in the search box and then the software examines the text looking for articles containing that specific word. A complex search might be called Advanced, Analytical, or Boolean as a software feature. Regardless of the name, the search feature allows the information seeker to key in multiple words in a search box joined by Boolean operators, typically AND, OR, and NOT. This type of search enables the information seeker to examine text for words that have a relationship. For example, students in Mrs. Hunter's class might want to find information about teenage drinking. If they searched on the topic of *alcoholism* they would find a significant list of articles in their hit list, only a small number of which might be about teenage drinking. However, if they used a complex search with the search phrase *alcoholism* AND *teenage*, the software would produce a hit list that was limited to articles that included references to both of those topics.

Information seekers and software producers refer to the search engine features of electronic resources by using different names that frequently have the same meaning. For example, people often talk about a *keyword search*. Sometimes this refers to the simple search feature that allows an information seeker to key in one word in a search box. In other situations, the reference is to a Boolean search. There are many similar examples of this confusing use of names for features in electronic information tools and resources, which makes using the software more challenging.

There are a growing number of search engines on the Web today. Consistency of terminology and function does not exist from one search engine to another. Information seekers are encouraged to use the Help features that are usually available with these search engines. If you use specific search engines frequently, you might want to make a print copy of the Help section for easy access to specific instructions. Chapter 4 has more information on using search engines.

Gathering Information from Authentic and Human Resources

Students engaged in inquiry-based learning often discover that they need to gather information from "authentic" sources. These sources include people who are experts in the chosen subject area, community information providers such as a land lab or a museum, or primary source documents (e.g., historical documents, letters, journals, logs, maps). This type of information access often requires students to be effective interviewers, so they should develop strategies to enable them to gather information from people.

Primary source documents are available from places like the historical society; and a rapidly growing collection is now on the Web. Primary source documents can provide very valuable information, but students must read these documents carefully with the understanding that the use of English is from another time period. Also, students should be aware that documents like letters, diaries, or journals can contain personal biases, so the information should be validated using another source.

Recording Information

The process of recording the information found during a search often defeats students, especially in today's information-rich learning environment. Students need to use the strategies of skimming and scanning to determine if the information they have located is even relevant to their research question or information need. As students attempt to determine this relevance, they should consider whether the information is fact or fiction, the accuracy and currency of the information, and whether the information came from a primary or secondary source. Students may find they need to recheck their information and validate it in one or two other sources. Recording bibliographic information requires students to identify the author, title, publisher and/or journal title, date, etc., so the source of the information is always clear. Many teachers require students to prepare bibliographies of their sources in a specific format based on a style manual.

Note taking is a strategy that can be done in a variety of formats. Sometimes students use the computer and a word processor to take notes. Teachers often request that students take notes using 3-by-5-inch note cards or paper of similar size because the cards can be arranged easily in the order that the information will appear in the finished paper.

It is important to remember that not all products today are research papers, which represents a linear organization of information. Teachers might want to provide students with different note-taking experiences so that they have strategies they can apply for the development of a product that is nonlinear. The students in Mrs. Hunter's class are taking notes using a T chart, which is a double-entry draft for recording information (see Table 1.2). On the left side of the paper, students record a summary of their information with at least a limited form of bibliographic information so their source is available. On the right side of the paper, students record their reflections about the information, including any ideas about the relevance of the information to their research question.

Table 1.2. T Chart for Summary and Reflection

Summaries of Notes	My Reflection
Hepatitis can be one result of alcohol and drug abuse. People who have more than two drinks a day often have this condition. (Johns Hopkins Health Information at www.intelihealth.com)	Check out what types of drinks cause this. Can two beers a day cause hepatitis? Or do you have to drink the hard stuff?
Alcohol abuse lots of times leads to other kinds of abuse. (Our school guidance counselor)	I think Mr. Tomlinson said this when he gave our class the usual speech before homecoming—go see him—see if he has anything to back this up.

INTERPRETATION

SCENARIO 1.4

Mrs. Reynolds's eighth-grade English class is studying mysteries and authors' writing techniques. The class is organized into several small groups, and the students in each group are reading a different mystery written by the same prominent mystery author. They have gathered some information on various techniques and styles authors use within the genre of mystery. Mrs. Reynolds has asked the students to keep a journal of the story elements (e.g. suspects, causes of death, alibis, detective strategies), as well as their reactions to the plot and character development, as they are reading their books.

In class discussions students have questioned the accuracy of some of these story elements, so they spent some time in the library media center trying to find information that would support or refute the statements. Each group created a timeline for their novel to show the sequence of events. They also created a comparison chart that analyzed the suspects and the clues related to each of them (see Figure 1.2). They used the chart to validate the information gathered from each of the characters in terms of conflicting information or supportive evidence for important clues.

Based on the evidence available in these comparison charts, Mrs. Reynolds asked the students to make a prediction about the solution of the mystery at various stages through the reading of the novel, with the final prediction occurring with only 20 pages left to be read. When students had finished reading their mystery books, Mrs. Reynolds asked each group to make a chart that analyzed the writing style and technique used by the author. Students presented this information to the full class using large poster paper so that comparisons could be made among the various books written by this mystery author. They also examined the timelines created by each group, looking for common patterns or themes that might support the notion that the author uses a formula for his or her writing.

Figure 1.2. Character and Clue Comparison Chart.

CLUES	Character #1	Character #2	Character #3	Character #4
1st Clue:				
2nd Clue:				
3rd Clue:				
4th Clue:				
5th Clue:				

The functions of the Interpretation stage are to assess the usefulness of the information and to develop a personal meaning. The Pathways model provides the following description of the Interpretation stage:

Information requires interpretation to become knowledge. The Interpretation stage engages searchers in the process of analyzing, synthesizing and evaluating information to determine its relevancy and usefulness to their research question or information need. Throughout this stage searchers reflect on the information they have gathered and construct personal meaning.

Interpretation is another very critical part of the research process, and, along with Presearch, one that is often neglected. Teachers do engage students in strategies of Interpretation, but this is often pursued in a shallow or hit-and-miss manner. Unfortunately, information seekers mistake information for knowledge; knowledge happens only as an individual constructs personal meaning from various bits of information. The Interpretation stage has less relevance and importance if the student's assignment or project does not require some level of critical thinking. A look-up assignment seldom requires students to engage in critical thinking but rather only to identify facts. The following sections discuss some specific strategies in the Interpretation stage.

Organizing Information

In our information-rich learning environment, students can often find much information about their topic, but the challenge is organizing the information into a framework to help them assess the usefulness of that information. The students in Mrs. Reynolds's class organized the information they acquired about their mystery novel by developing a timeline, a character and clue comparison chart, and a list of story elements.

The timeline and comparison charts are graphic organizers, which can be very useful tools for organizing information. Comparison charts can be set up in columns to compare two concepts or in multiple columns to compare a variety of concepts. Sometimes information becomes clearer if it is organized into classifications or categories. Venn diagrams help students discern how some concepts are related to others or perhaps not related. Another strategy for organizing information is paraphrasing. Teachers are often frustrated with students who simply copy information they find in resources and turn that in as their report. This behavior is enabled by the use of look-up assignments or topic assignments that are very general. Teachers must first set up assignments and projects that are driven by questions that foster inquiry and critical thinking, then require students to record their information by using paraphrasing and a limited number of quotations, which must be referenced with sources.

Higher-Level Thinking Strategies

Interpretation requires higher-level thinking strategies such as analyzing; comparing and contrasting; classifying; evaluating; drawing conclusions; synthesizing; and determining themes, patterns, or trends. These strategies enable students to carefully examine their information and ultimately construct their own personal meaning.

The students in Mrs. Reynolds's class analyzed the plot elements of the mystery novel they read by comparing the clues that were related to each of the main characters. Their analysis enabled them to uncover differences in the stories told by each of the characters. This analytical process also pointed out similarities in the characters' stories, which required students to decide whether the evidence was substantiating or incriminating. Ultimately, this process can enable students to draw conclusions and make predictions to solve the crime.

The timeline developed by Mrs. Reynolds's students enabled them to see the sequence of events. A similar timeline developed by character would allow students to uncover controversial evidence from one character to another.

Mrs. Reynolds asked her students to evaluate the information they found in the story in the form of clues. When they questioned the accuracy of clues or other plot elements, she asked them to find information that would either support or refute the information used by the author.

At the conclusion of the mystery unit, the students analyzed the plot elements of each of the novels written by the same author, looking for patterns that might suggest the author's writing technique was based on a formula or whether the author is a very creative mystery writer.

Filtering Information

When students evaluate information, they need to apply some filtering strategies that enable them to assess issues such as point of view or bias. Bias is often reflected in information available today, yet students tend to accept information they find as fact merely because it appears in print or on the Web. Requiring students to have two different sources of information to support a perspective they want to use in a final report at least reduces the chances that the perspective is a totally biased point of view. Another strategy is to require students to find information that reflects two or more perspectives on their topic.

It's also important for students to consider that there are several perspectives or points of view about a subject or a concept and to respect those points of view. When students are asked to solve a problem, often the solution process requires them to understand all points of view and employ compromise and negotiation to develop a viable solution.

Ethical Use of Information

Ethical use of information is founded on the principle of intellectual property rights. Knowledge has become a commodity, and people own the knowledge they have created in the same way individuals or companies own other types of property. The copyright law protects the intellectual property rights of people and companies. This notion of intellectual property as a commodity is going to be common in the world that the young people of today will inherit, so it is very important for students to understand and practice the ethical use of information. This means that when they use text, graphics, sound, pictures, and so forth that others have created, they must give credit to those other authors or creators. It is also important for students to understand that only a small portion of a work can be used without permission from the author or creator.

A part of ethical use of information is using and respecting information in a responsible manner. This strategy also appears in the Communication stage, where students should practice ethical use of information as they complete their projects.

COMMUNICATION

SCENARIO 1.5

Emily, Robin, Dylan, and Tad are working on a project about children in Colonial America. Their teacher, Mr. Pierce, asked them what they thought life was like for children living in the early colonies of America. All the students in the class brainstormed a list of questions they wanted to know about children living in that time, broke their questions into clusters of related topics, and divided into small groups based on those topics. Emily, Robin, Dylan, and Tad chose to research the home life of children in Colonial America, including things like their clothing, the foods they ate, and entertainment.

Each group gathered information and used graphic organizers to organize and analyze their information. As a large group they talked about the best way to present their information. Emily's group decided to create an authentic journal of a 10-year-old girl living in Plymouth Colony. Other small groups decided to write a newspaper and create a diorama. Two groups worked together to write a short skit. Another group focused on schools in Colonial America and decided to create an art exhibit of pictures showing scenes from an early schoolroom.

When the students were finished with their projects, Mr. Pierce arranged for them to present them to two other fifth-grade classes that were also studying Colonial America. He told the audience that the students had tried to represent the time period and the experiences of those colonial children in a historically accurate manner. At the end of each small group's presentation, he asked the audience if there was any information they thought was historically inaccurate. The next day he asked the students in each small group to do a self- and peer evaluation of their projects based on the appropriateness of the format used to present the information.

The function of the Communication stage is to construct and present the new knowledge. In this stage information seekers can apply their information and share their new knowledge. The Pathways model provides the following description of the Communication stage:

> *The Communication stage allows searchers to organize, apply, and present new knowledge relevant to their research question or information need. They choose a format that appropriately reflects the new knowledge they need to convey, then plan and create their product.*

Applying Information and Sharing New Knowledge

When searchers have gathered information and constructed new knowledge, their next step is to apply that knowledge in some manner. Too often students are led to believe that the conclusion of a project is to write a paper or give a report. It is important for students to understand that their new knowledge may allow them to answer a question or solve a problem.

For the next step of presenting the information to others, students must make decisions about an appropriate format. In many situations, teachers decide the format, but giving students the opportunity to make that decision based on their understanding of the information they want to present and the format that will most appropriately represent the information allows them to apply critical thinking skills. The Pathways model provides a list of formats by categories (e.g., visual, visual/motion, text, oral, and multimedia).

Teachers are encouraged to provide students with learning experiences that will give them the skills to create a variety of the formats shown on the model until students develop a repertoire of these skills through their years of schooling. Initially, younger students could be allowed to choose among a limited number of formats for presenting their new knowledge. As they grow older and more experienced with the production and creation of various formats, their choices will expand until, as high school students, they should be free to make their own decisions. Self-evaluation and teacher assessment of projects should include a focus on the appropriateness of the presentation format.

The students in Mr. Pierce's class made decisions about how they wanted to present their new knowledge about the lives of children in Colonial America. Their choices are interesting because they included text, visual, and oral presentations. The appropriateness of their format choices was evaluated through both a peer- and self-evaluation process.

EVALUATION

SCENARIO 1.6

Miss Rivard's high school civics class is investigating how the news media influence local and state elections. These students have used the Pathways model for previous research projects and have a good understanding of the process. During one class session they brainstormed a list of potential problems and issues related to the media's role in the electoral process. Students spent some time building background knowledge until they felt they were ready to write their specific research questions. Miss Rivard asked students to keep reflective journals focusing on the information they were gathering and their reactions to that information. She also asked them to keep a log of their research process clearly showing the stages and strategies they followed using the Pathways model.

Working in small groups, the students began to search for information with a strong focus on local newspapers, television, and radio news programs. They interviewed journalists, candidates, campaign managers, and people who were potential voters. Students regularly used graphic organizers and made decisions about which organizer they might use to support various strategies in their process.

Periodically throughout this project, Miss Rivard, and Mr. Quinn, the library media specialist, met with small groups of students to check on their progress. Students analyzed news reports and compared various points of view. Miss Rivard and her students considered the most appropriate format for using their new knowledge, and they decided to hold a debate with students taking opposing sides on issues related to the news media and elections. They invited several members of the news media to be an audience for this debate and asked them to evaluate the results of the debate when it was concluded. The next day, after the debate, Miss Rivard requested that students bring their logs and journals to class. She asked them to write a reflection on their research process, responding to the question, "What were the most challenging parts of this research assignment, and how would you overcome those challenges with another research project?"

The function of the Evaluation stage is thinking about the process and product of a research process. The Pathways model provides the following description of the Evaluation stage:

> *Evaluation (self and peer) is ongoing in this nonlinear information process model and should occur throughout each stage. Searchers use their evaluation of the process to make revisions that enable them to develop their own unique information seeking process. It is through this continuous evaluation and revision process that searchers develop the ability to become independent searchers. Searchers also evaluate their product or the results of their communication of new knowledge.*

Evaluation has typically been regarded as related to student projects, but there has been little focus on their research process. Although self- and peer evaluation of the products that students create is important, equal attention must be given to the process.

Evaluation is a critical part of the research process because information seekers can grow and develop with the process only if they have opportunities to reflect on their research experiences. Learning is a process of building on past learning experiences, reflecting on both successes and failures, and applying that knowledge to new learning experiences. If students are to become independent learners, they must use the Pathways model with many research projects, reflect on their process, and apply the knowledge they gain from each experience to the next project and information need.

Evaluation of process should be ongoing throughout all of the Pathways stages. The students in Miss Rivard's class used journals to reflect on the information they were gathering and the new knowledge they were constructing. They used logs to keep track of their research process. Graphic organizers were available for students at various stages, and both Miss Rivard and Mr. Quinn used these as they facilitated the evaluation process by students. The final reflection question that Miss Rivard asked students to write on caused them to examine the challenges they encountered and to think about other strategies they might use in future searches. The process of reflection is an important part of self-evaluation of process.

REFERENCES

Note: All Web addresses accessed December 21, 2001.

AASL and AECT. (1998). *Information literacy standards for student learning.* Chicago: American Library Association.

2001 Grolier multimedia encyclopedia. (2001). Danbury, CT: Grolier.

Readers' guide to periodical literature. (2001). Bronx, NY: H. W. Wilson.

SIRS Researcher®. Boca Raton, FL: SIRS. [Online]. Available: http://www.sirs.com /products/rfeatures.htm

WEB RESOURCES

Note: All Web addresses accessed December 21, 2001.

Alta Vista. (2001). [Online]. Available: http://www.altavista.com/

Google. (2001). [Online]. Available: http://www.google.com/

Look Smart. (2001). [Online]. Available: http://www.looksmart.com

NativeWeb. (1994–2001). [Online]. Available: http://www.nativeweb.org/

Web of Addictions. (1995–2000). Produced by Andrew L. Homer and Dick Dillon. [Online]. Available: http://www.well.com/user/woa

Yahoo. (2001). [Online]. Available: http://www.yahoo.com

Yahooligans. (2001). [Online]. Available: http://www.yahooligans.com

Inquiry and the Pathways Model

What is inquiry learning, and what does it look like in practice? How do library media specialists and classroom teachers integrate an information process model like Pathways to Knowledge with inquiry learning? With these questions in mind, it seemed appropriate to first develop a scenario that shows students engaged in inquiry learning and using the Pathways model as a practical framework to illustrate the principles of inquiry learning. As you read the scenario at the beginning of this chapter, keep in mind that the discussion of inquiry learning that follows frequently refers back to it. The scenario is based on a Heroes unit, and that Heroes Planning Guide is included in Appendix B (see Figure B.1).

SCENARIO 2.1

Heroes Unit

The middle school students in Mrs. Sanchez's class had enthusiastically participated in the panel discussion with several guest athletes from their local university who were popular and successful. Five athletes (two basketball players, one football player, one volleyball player, and one swimmer) came to talk with students. The primary focus of this discussion was the challenges of being perceived as a hero by campus students and many others in the extended university community. The athletes, two women and three men, each spoke for a short time about their lives and what had happened along the way to help them be successful. Students asked perceptive questions about differences between sports and also about gender. For example, they wanted to know if the male basketball player was considered more of a hero than the female player and how each felt about that perception. They also discussed the athletes' ideas about personal characteristics of athlete heroes in relation to some of the nationally recognized athletes.

The next day Mrs. Sanchez and her students met in the library media center. She asked students to work in small groups to brainstorm a list of heroes. The class then came back together as a large group and constructed a web based on their brainstormed list of heroes. They organized the web by job or professional category (e.g., sports figures, artists, musicians, government leaders, film stars). Mr. Thomas, the library media specialist, talked with students about resources they might use to develop their background knowledge about heroes. They spent some time gathering information and expanding their list of heroes. Mrs.

Sanchez asked students what they might like to know about these heroes and how they might proceed with this inquiry unit. As their inquiry into heroes developed, students frequently made reflective entries in journals and engaged in small group discussions that led them to question their knowledge about heroes and the new information they were finding.

After spending several days in the library media center, the students decided they would each investigate two heroes. Their research questions would be: (1) Who are these people, and what has made them famous? (2) What (if any) life-changing events occurred in the lives of these people? (3) Why are these people special? In addition, the students formed small groups that would each be responsible for developing a common list of characteristics about their individual heroes. As a final activity, groups would present their list of hero characteristics and the large group would reach consensus on one list of shared characteristics.

Students gathered information, wrote journal entries about their information and inquiry process, continually evaluated information, and held periodic small group discussions about the characteristics of heroes. As their work progressed, they decided to do presentations about their heroes and invite parents and community people. They organized their information, used timelines to visually show the events of a hero's life, and created storyboards to design their presentations.

Mrs. Sanchez suggested they use a rubric to evaluate the presentations; she and the students spent part of one class period constructing the rubric (see Figure B.2 in Appendix B). The students thought that the resulting rubric helped them understand how to develop a quality presentation. On the day of the presentations, the class list of hero characteristics was posted in the front of the classroom. As students presented information about their heroes, Mrs. Sanchez engaged the audience and students in discussions about how their characteristics were reflected in the heroes they were presenting.

On the final day of their heroes inquiry unit, students wrote a response in their journals to the question, "How do heroes influence my life?" which allowed them to demonstrate their understanding of their research questions.

When we were in school, typically our teachers gave us a reading assignment in our textbook. Most class time was spent listening to a lecture. Depending on the class, there would be some discussion, but the focus was on providing the "right" answers. Debate was not typically encouraged. We often had worksheets to complete with fill-in questions that required information from our textbook. We gave reports on topics assigned by the teacher and we gathered that information from the textbook, library books, or magazines. Tests were usually multiple choice or fill-in-the blank questions, with an occasional essay question. We realize our school memories may be older than yours, but we suspect this scenario is still being repeated in some schools today.

The traditional approach described here is based on behaviorist learning theory and has affected curriculum and instruction for many years (see Figure 2.1, page 26). Behaviorists suggest that there is a confined body of knowledge that can be taught and tested; hence, there are definite right and wrong answers to questions. Traditional teachers impart knowledge, and students are considered vessels to be filled, which is a passive approach to learning. Traditional curricula are written with behavioral objectives, and the primary resources are textbooks and teacher lectures. Evaluation is typically based on objective tests. Behavioral objectives tend to foster fragmentation, and the curriculum is often broad and shallow. Usually there is little higher-level thinking in the traditional curriculum. Much of the traditional curriculum is focused on the knowledge or fact level, with memorization of knowledge.

Mrs. Sanchez's students (Scenario 2.1) are studying heroes. In a traditional hero unit, students might typically select a hero from a list generated by the teacher. Each student would write a report or perhaps give a presentation about this hero, but little activity would engage them in thinking critically about the hero characteristics or how those characteristics might relate to their own lives.

Constructivist learning theory, developed by cognitive psychologists, suggests that learning is "the active building of knowledge through dynamic interaction with information and experience. Cognitive psychologists define learning itself as the active building of knowledge through dynamic interaction with information and experience" (AASL and AECT, 1998, p. 2). Constructivists believe that we have a schema in our brains, and we learn by making connections to prior knowledge, constructing new understandings, and connecting those to our schema. Much of the new perspective on brain-based learning supports this learning theory.

Contemporary curriculum design is based on constructivism and engages students in active and student-centered learning experiences. Common characteristics are apparent across all types of contemporary curriculum design. "These characteristics are: critical thinking, authentic context, depth of content knowledge, learner choice and engagement, and interactive knowledge construction" (Pappas, 1998, p. 29).

Learning Theory

Behaviorism

Constructivism

Traditional curriculum design is characterized by:

Constructivist curriculum design is characterized by:

- teacher as knowledge provider
- student as passive learner
- curriculum as a confined body of knowledge
- objective evaluation (i.e., tests)

- teacher as guide
- student as active learner
- curriculum that reflects essential understandings
- authentic assessment (i.e., performance demonstrations)

© 2002 Pappas and Tepe

Figure 2.1. Learning Theory.

This perspective can be found in various contemporary approaches to curriculum design including authentic learning, problem-based learning, student-centered learning, and discovery learning. Figure 2.2, page 28, shows these curriculum design approaches falling under the umbrella of constructivism with the support of learning styles, brain-based learning, multiple intelligences, and inquiry. Authentic learning has become a common reference to curriculum design that involves students in problem solving and projects that are related to the real world.

The students in Mrs. Sanchez's class are studying heroes, a student-centered unit that engages them in meaningful choices and presents them with opportunities to construct their own knowledge. Students are actively involved in identifying heroes, developing research questions, making decisions about a plan for gathering information, and using consensus to develop a master set of hero characteristics.

INQUIRY LEARNING

Inquiry learning is a foundation element of constructivist learning theory and authentic curriculum design. *Information Power* states that "the information search process mirrors this description of the learning process: students actively seek to construct meaning from the sources they encounter and to create products that shape and communicate that meaning effectively" (AASL and AECT, 1998, p. 2).

Inquiry is an investigative process that engages students in answering questions, solving real world problems, confronting issues, or exploring personal interests. The notion of inquiry appears in many educational disciplines. Karen Sheingold (1987), Director of the Center for Children and Technology at the Bank Street College of Education, suggests that "(i)nquiry is a complex process that includes formulating a problem or question, searching through and/or collecting information to address the problem or question, making sense of that information, and developing an understanding of, point of view about, or 'answer' to the question" (p. 81). Joy McGregor (1999) suggests that "inquiry learning is also known as discovery learning [and] . . . is typically student-centered, with teachers acting as guides and coaches rather than as knowledge providers" (p. 34). Mary Dalbotten (1998) believes "the overall process requires that students apply analysis, synthesis, and evaluation skills as they find and use information and make generalizations." Even though the steps appear to be linear, "in actuality they are cyclical or recursive . . . inquiry in real life is messy and chaotic" (p. 32).

Inquiry requires students to be active rather than passive learners, which means that teachers and library media specialists must engage them in a learning task that allows meaningful choices. There is a social context to inquiry learning in the sense that students need opportunities to discuss and share new ideas. Such discussions allow students to discover new ideas, see relationships between ideas, and build new knowledge in ways that might not be possible if students were left to learn on their own (Pappas, 2000).

Inquiry learning has four important elements—learner engagement, questioning, applying an information process, and constructing new understandings—which are practiced by learners within a learning community. A learning community is composed of learners, both children and adults; knowledgeable resource people; and information resources. (See Figure 2.3, page 29.)

Figure 2.2. Contemporary Curriculum Design.

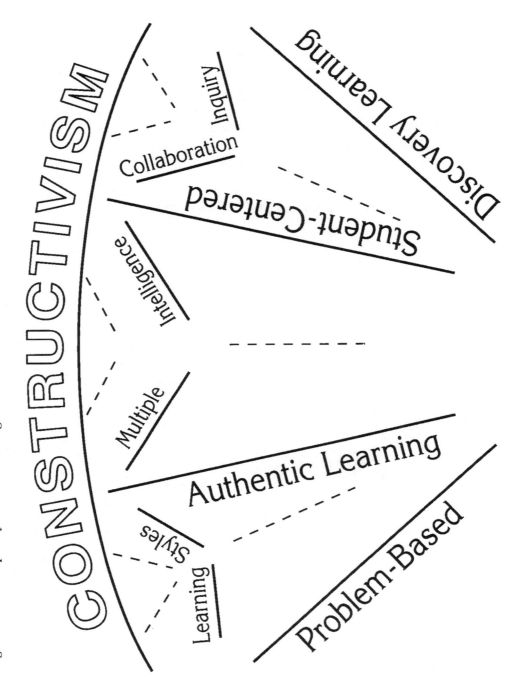

© 2002 Pappas and Tepe

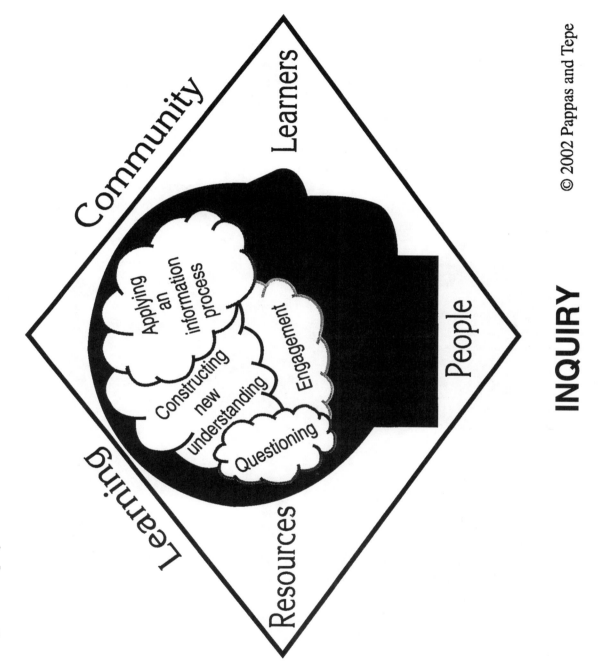

Figure 2.3. Inquiry.

Community

Learners

Learning

Resources

People

Applying an information process

Constructing new understanding

Engagement

Questioning

INQUIRY

© 2002 Pappas and Tepe

Inquiry begins as an individual becomes engaged and pursues a problem that needs resolution or a personal interest or issue. Students who pursue inquiry must have ownership of the problem or issue rather than having that problem be imposed upon them by a teacher. Questioning permeates inquiry. In the early stages of inquiry, a student focuses on "What do I already know or want to know about my issue or problem?" Applying an information process allows students to gather, evaluate, and use new information. As students move deeper into inquiry, a recursive process ensues as they gather information, question, and reflect, then gather information again, questioning, synthesizing, and evaluating until they have successfully constructed new knowledge.

Questioning transcends all components of inquiry learning. Students should be encouraged to frequently raise new questions that surface as a result of the information they have been gathering. Questioning can be fostered by teachers and library media specialists through coaching activities. This might mean providing students with writing prompts or the use of models that lead to questions (Rankin, 1999). As students become more adept at this questioning process, they should be encouraged to develop questions without prompts from teachers (Pappas, 2000).

INQUIRY LEARNING IN PRACTICE

Inquiry learning is student centered, which means that students have ownership in the process rather than pursuing a project that has been assigned by the teacher. The students in Mrs. Sanchez's class (Scenario 2.1) became interested in heroes following a panel discussion in their classroom with several prominent university athletes. With some coaching and facilitating by their teacher, these students began to pursue an inquiry project about heroes. Unlike some hero units, in this one the students planned to go beyond the investigation of one hero into a class profile of hero characteristics developed through collaboration and consensus. Critical thinking therefore became an important focus.

Questioning, including reflection, is an element of inquiry learning. Brainstorming and webbing are useful strategies to enhance questioning in the early stage of inquiry. The students in Mrs. Sanchez's class worked in small groups to develop webs focused on types of heroes and then specific heroes. They used their webbed information to develop several research questions to follow as they gathered information about individual heroes. As their inquiry process developed, students engaged in questioning through reflective journal writing, small group discussions, and consensus building. Questioning and reflection are skills that must be developed through practice. "Teachers and library media specialists can foster this questioning and reflection by using prompts" (Pappas, 2000, p. 29). Examples of prompts that Mrs. Sanchez provided for her students include the following questions:

♦ What was the most important thing you learned today?

♦ Was there any information you found that surprised you? Why?

♦ How does the information you located today answer your research question?

♦ If the information you located today does not answer your research question, what is your next step? (Pappas, 2000, p. 29)

Inquiry requires students to find information from many different information providers and resources. The learning community is important as students look for information beyond the walls of their school. The students in Mrs. Sanchez's class used a variety of tools in their school library, including periodical databases, the catalog, and Web tools like directories and search engines. Many students wanted to have a personal interview with their heroes. Sometimes the hero was a local person, and the interview could take place in person or on the telephone. In other cases the hero was a national figure and not easily available by telephone or in person. The Web has a variety of options for contacting prominent people. Sometimes e-mail exchanges or chat room interactions can be arranged.

Primary source documents can be found at local historical societies, government offices, museums, historical landmarks and parks, and on the Web. There are often Web sites about heroes such as George Washington or Abraham Lincoln where personal or professional documents are available. The Library of Congress's American Memory Project includes a significant number of primary source documents. Mrs. Sanchez's students planned their search strategies, identified appropriate keywords, initiated searches, evaluated the results, recorded new information, and evaluated their information for accuracy, biases, and relevance to their research questions.

Using information and constructing new understandings requires students to engage in reflection and critical thinking. "Reflection is a process of thinking about what you know, questioning new information, making connections to prior knowledge, or evaluating information" (Pappas, 2000). Rankin (1999) believes that "the daily use of a journal is one of the best ways to build metacognition in a research project" (p. 44). Students also should organize their information so they can look for patterns, trends, sequences, and contrasts, then analyze and evaluate. To compare characteristics of heroes, students in Mrs. Sanchez's class used timelines and Venn diagrams. Their final activity was to construct a list of hero characteristics that they developed through consensus, a task that involved organizing their information, synthesis, evaluation, and negotiation skills.

INQUIRY AND PATHWAYS TO KNOWLEDGE

The Pathways model provides the information process and thus the strategies that students need as they pursue inquiry. Inquiry learning and Pathways represent a recursive, nonlinear learning experience, which is underscored on the graphic version with the band effect and arrows between stages with double arrowheads (see Figure A.1 in Appendix A). Questioning, including reflection and evaluation, is an important element within inquiry learning, and this element appears as a strategy on the Pathways model.

When the students in Mrs. Sanchez's class listened to the university athletes and asked them questions, they were showing curiosity, which is part of the Appreciation stage of the Pathways model. These students brainstormed a list of heroes and constructed a web. Both brainstorming and webbing are Presearch strategies. They developed research questions—also a Presearch strategy. Students gathered information and used strategies from the Search stage. They made the decision to give presentations about their heroes that required them to organize their information and use timelines—strategies that fall within the Communication stage. When they gave their presentations they used a rubric the class had helped to develop as a tool for both peer- and self-evaluation—strategies in the Evaluation stage.

Rubrics are an important assessment tool for inquiry learning. They provide a "precise and concrete description of successful performance. A rubric is a scaled set of criteria that clearly defines for the student and the teacher what a range of acceptable and unacceptable performance looks like" (Donham, 1998, p. 9). The North Carolina Department of Public Instruction has a Web site that includes a section on constructing rubrics that you might find useful. An example of a rubric is Figure B.2 in Appendix B.

INQUIRY LEARNING CHANGES TRADITIONAL ROLES

Inquiry learning changes the roles of students and teachers. Teachers (i.e., classroom teachers, library media specialists, special teachers, etc.) become coaches, facilitators, and tutors. The teacher as coach monitors the learning activities of students and interacts with students to keep them on track. Sometimes that interaction takes the form of asking probing questions to foster critical thinking, or perhaps guiding consideration of an idea or concept related to their research topic that had been overlooked. A coach's role is not to tell students what to do but rather to nudge them so they can figure things out for themselves.

In a coaching role, the library media specialist might prepare a pathfinder that would help students locate information rather than pull all the resources on a topic and put them on a cart. The primary role of the facilitator is to remove impediments or roadblocks so learning can occur. Depending on the age of the students, a facilitator must anticipate potential problems and find solutions. As a facilitator, a library media specialist might provide mini-classes or written instructions for using databases so that students could use the technology on an as-needed basis rather than demonstrating the use of the database to all students regardless of whether they have a need.

In her facilitator role, Mrs. Sanchez (Scenario 2.1) arranged for the guest athletes to visit in the classroom. She also worked collaboratively with Mr. Thomas, the library media specialist, to help students with the search part of their unit. In a tutoring role, teachers and library media specialists might work one-on-one with a student teaching specific searching strategies or following the format for a bibliographic entry. Figure 2.4, page 34, shows the changing roles of a teacher (classroom teacher, library media specialist) in inquiry learning.

The students' roles also change. In inquiry learning, students are responsible for establishing the focus of their research and developing research questions. Learning that is student-centered requires some form of meaningful mental engagement on the part of the student. Giving students choices means we also expect them to deal with the consequences of their decisions, although there is some type of safety net in place. Inquiry learning engages students in social interaction and small group work. Students who have no experience working in groups often cause dysfunctional groups. Some type of training for cooperative learning should take place, provided by the teacher in a coaching role.

Figure 2.4. Inquiry Learning Changes Roles.

Inquiry Learning Changes Roles

No longer is learning an experience that is poured into the learner by a teacher but rather the learner is now responsible for constructing his or her own personal meaning. That means learners have a decision making role in the development of the learning plan. Collaboration and interactivity become important activities in the learning process. (Pappas, 1999a, pp. 28–29)

Learner	Teacher
The learner . . .	The teacher . . .
is actively engaged in learning	designs curriculum that effectively engages learners and is based on core understandings
independently follows a process to locate, use, and evaluate information to construct new knowledge	facilitates the learning process by establishing a learning environment that enables learners to be independent
engages in interaction with other learners to enable knowledge construction	acts as a coach by posing provocative questions that guide learners to think critically and reach a depth of content knowledge
works collaboratively with other learners	enables the authentic assessment of the inquiry process and learner products
gathers information using the multiple resources of the learning community	facilitates and coaches collaborative learning experiences
values all forms of literature and creative expression	works collaboratively with the LMS and other classroom teachers to plan, implement, and evaluate authentic learning
practices ethical behavior when using information or technology	facilitates connections with the learning community
engages her/his natural sense of curiosity to solve problems or gather information about personal interests	fosters an appreciation for curiosity, discovery, literature, and other forms of creative expression
self-evaluates the inquiry process and any products	

MANAGING THE
INQUIRY LEARNING ENVIRONMENT

The learning environment in a traditional school tends to be closed, with limited connection to the community. Teachers instruct in their self-contained classrooms and tend to view themselves as self-sufficient when providing students with resources beyond the information available in their textbooks. In a constructivist classroom, the learning environment is open, with many connections to the learning community. It is important for teachers to understand that the shift from a traditional classroom to one that is constructivist and authentic does not happen overnight but rather takes time and experience. There is an intermediary stage that we label "thematic." A thematic curriculum design may incorporate some of the elements of authentic learning but not all and may reflect some of the characteristics of constructivism.

Typically, a unit revolves around a theme, students have some choice in their learning activities, and they engage in gathering information from multiple resources. Often, the unit focuses on disparate activities that are theme-based and lack a focus on the big ideas usually reflected in essential questions. Authentic learning involves critical thinking, depth of content knowledge, meaningful student choice, an authentic context, interactive knowledge construction, and the application of information-seeking as a process (Pappas, 1999a).

A learning community is "the global web of individuals and organizations who are interconnected in a lifelong quest to understand and meet constantly changing information needs" (AASL and AECT, 1998, p. 48). It holds the learner at the center, "but all people engaged in the community have the potential to be learners and teachers" (Pappas, 1999b, p. 30). Technology has greatly enhanced the learning potential within a learning community by enabling connections with information, experts, teachers, and other learners around the world.

Students who engage in inquiry need access to quality resources and information, and it is important that this access be available as their needs require. Flexible access to the library media center is an important requirement in a learning community. However, there are also other information providers within the learning community, such as the public library, local museums, the historical society, or a nature preserve. People are an important resource, and these might be experts on the Web, members of the local government, or grandparents who can provide a personal historical perspective. Primary source documents take on a special importance when students pursue an inquiry project, because these enable a connection with the real world. They may be available nearby, at the local historical society but also on the Web. Documents include letters, personal papers, diaries, legal documents, ship manifests, and so forth.

An open environment can make learning come alive for students, but there are also challenges that must be handled by teachers in their role as facilitator. For example, authentic learning experiences can be enhanced if students can go to a museum, the historical society, the mayor's office, and similar places, but these field trips are sometimes difficult to facilitate. The challenge teachers and library media specialists face is providing these authentic experiences without engaging in large numbers of field trips (Pappas, 2000).

All members of the learning community must work together to make these learning experiences happen. Teachers, working collaboratively with the library media specialist, might take part of a class to visit the local newspaper, while the rest of the class gathers information in the library media center. The cordless telephone, speakerphones, and teleconferencing also enable conversations with community people without requiring the complications of a field trip.

Parents, grandparents, and other members of the community will find the notion of a learning community very different from their school experiences. Involving community members in the inquiry learning experiences of students results in a two-fold reward. First, they can actually benefit from involvement with students who are working on an inquiry project. Students learn from the community members, and those adults might learn something from the students. Second, asking (for example) an editor from the local newspaper to visit the school and talk with a small group of students allows for an exchange of information without the complications of transporting those students off the school grounds. Also, the school visit allows the editor (or any community member) to see excited students engaged in a meaningful learning experience.

The part of inquiry learning that seems to be most challenging for teachers is the fact that their students will all be working on different projects and will be responsible for acquiring slightly different content knowledge. In short, they will not all be on the same page in the textbook at the same time. A traditional teacher's first question is, "How will I manage this?"

One strategy is to put students into small, collaborative learning groups. Organizing groups of students so that they are all working on the same task or project does not guarantee that learning is taking place. A mistake that teachers often make is assuming that students know how to function in small groups, and they may not. Collaborative learning requires teaching students group skills; for example, the role of a leader in the small group, delegating tasks to group members, listening, and respecting the ideas of others. *Cooperative Learning* (Kagan, 1994) is an excellent resource that teachers can use to help students be more productive in small groups.

Students typically do not know how to plan and organize their learning. Teachers who are successful with inquiry learning often use different types of organizers to help students put structure into their learning. For example, the students in Mrs. Sanchez's class created webs to organize their initial brainstorming information. Sometimes teachers encourage students to gather initial background information and then expand their webs into mind maps. Students were journaling throughout the Heroes unit in Scenario 2.1. As students began to plan their inquiry strategy, the information in their journals could be used within this planning process.

Mrs. Sanchez's students used timelines and Venn diagrams to establish a sequence of events and to compare the characteristics of their heroes. Organizers might also fall in the category of advance organizers. An advance organizer establishes some structure for organizing information without requiring prescribed responses. For example, a search log is an advance organizer. Over time, students should develop an understanding of which organizers they need for specific tasks, a skill that ultimately enables them to become independent learners. There are some excellent organizer Web sites, and several are included in the resource list at www.pathwaysmodel.com/resources/weblinks/.

Planning is another important aspect of managing the inquiry learning environment. Collaboration requires teachers and library media specialists to plan together so all will know their roles in the unit. Collaboration is more than identifying resources for a unit; it involves co-teaching.

Students should engage in planning activities if they are making decisions about their own learning. It is important for them to see their teachers planning and working together because that provides them with a model for their own behavior. Planning must include an element of flexibility, because inquiry learning is nonlinear and students might need to return to an element of the inquiry process. For example, the questioning process often uncovers a missing piece or a broader perspective, causing students to change their plan. A checklist is a useful organizer that allows students to track their progress in relation to their plan.

DESIGNING AN INQUIRY UNIT

Because inquiry learning requires student buy-in, motivating students' curiosity to a level that has the potential to actively engage them in the inquiry process becomes a high priority. Mrs. Sanchez (Scenario 2.1) used the panel discussion with prominent local athletes. There are many strategies teachers can use to begin an inquiry learning unit, and sometimes the problem, or students themselves, will raise topics for inquiry. Some of these strategies are reading a compelling story, posing an intriguing problem, or viewing a gripping video.

An inquiry unit requires collaboration between the teacher and library media specialist. Typically, some form of planning guide is used. (An example of a planning guide for Scenario 2.1 is Figure B.1 in Appendix B.) An initial planning session took place between Mrs. Sanchez and Mr. Thomas, the library media specialist. Working together, they developed the essential understandings and questions for the unit and the assessment criteria. In this type of collaborative planning, Mr. Thomas might have been the one who suggested they begin the unit by asking the university athletes to visit and participate in a panel discussion. At this stage an initial time frame of three weeks could be established for the unit, with the understanding that student needs and interests might bring about some adjustment in time.

Mr. Thomas agreed to an initial search for information about those heroes that have often appealed to students in past units. He suggested they bookmark some Web sites to help facilitate student background information searches. Both Mrs. Sanchez and Mr. Thomas were in agreement that journaling should be an important part of the unit. Mrs. Sanchez asked Mr. Thomas if students could hold their brainstorming session in the library media center, with both of them facilitating the exercise, and Mr. Thomas agreed. They scheduled another planning session after the fourth day of the unit. At this point, both teachers thought that they would have a sense of the additional needs students might have in terms of mini-lessons and tutoring requirements.

At the next planning session, Mr. Thomas volunteered to help read journals and meet with several of the small groups for discussions. He suggested that mini-lessons on keyword searching; evaluating information for relevance, accuracy, bias, and currency; and use of graphic organizers would be useful for students. Mr. Thomas also suggested that he teach a review session on *Electric Library* and *SIRS Researcher* for those students who needed extra help. Mrs. Sanchez stressed the importance of engaging students in a questioning process as they gathered information. They both talked about using the journals to support the questioning process. Mrs. Sanchez said students wanted to give presentations about their heroes and use both *PowerPoint*® (2001) and *HyperStudio*® (2001). They decided to invite the technology teacher, Mrs. Allen, to their next meeting.

Another planning session was held several days later, and Mrs. Allen joined them. They talked about the need for students to use a storyboard to plan their presentations. Mrs. Allen said students had learned to use *PowerPoint* in their last computer mini-course, and she thought that they could probably create the presentations they needed with only minimal review. She thought they should concentrate on *PowerPoint* rather than trying to help students use both programs. Mrs. Sanchez and Mr. Thomas agreed. They made arrangements for students to have access to the computer lab for several days. They also talked about assessment strategies and tools. Mrs. Sanchez suggested they engage the students in developing a rubric that could be used for peer- and self-assessment of their presentations. They discussed some primary criteria for the rubric so they would be able to guide the conversation with students. Mrs. Sanchez asked Mrs. Allen to participate in the rubric development exercise with students. Mr. Thomas and Mrs. Sanchez discussed their strategy for facilitating the consensus-building activity for developing a composite list of hero characteristics.

At an informal hall meeting several days later with Mr. Thomas, Mrs. Sanchez asked if students could give their presentations in the library media center. She had invited parents and some local community people to be in the audience for these presentations. She also asked Mr. Thomas if they could videotape the presentations, and he agreed.

When the unit was completed, all three teachers met to evaluate it. They decided to brainstorm a list of the positives about the unit as well as suggestions for change. Mrs.

Sanchez had asked her students to evaluate the unit, and their feedback was included in the lists. Student feedback varied about the opening activity of the unit. Some students really enjoyed the opportunity to meet with athletes from the university but wondered if it would be possible to involve some professional athletes in the future. Other students thought there was too much emphasis on athletes at that stage. All three teachers agreed that the unit was worth repeating in another year.

CHANGING LEARNING

The inquiry learning process described in this chapter represents change across the educational community. One or two people might initiate the change process, but systemic change requires collaborative efforts and buy-in from library media specialists, teachers, principals, curriculum directors, and superintendents. Changing from a traditional curriculum to one that is authentic will require several years of incremental changes to the design of curriculum, instructional strategies used by teachers, schedules of students in both elementary and secondary schools to allow for flexible and open access to school libraries and technology, and planning time.

This change process can be a challenge in today's standards-based environment. Many state standards have been written using goals that reflect critical thinking and problem solving. There is a great deal of pressure for students to score well on the state tests based on these standards. In this situation, inquiry learning has great potential to help students be more successful on the tests because this type of learning focuses on higher levels of thinking and gives students opportunities to practice problem solving and critical thinking. However, some state standards are still focused on the knowledge level of learning, with a very specific focus on facts. Making the shift to inquiry learning will be difficult when that is the case.

Making the change to inquiry learning requires significant time spent in professional development for teachers because inquiry learning is fundamentally a different way of teaching. It means changing the learning environment in classrooms and the school. It may mean shifting some monies now earmarked for textbook adoptions to multiple resources and technology for classrooms and the school library. Making the change requires adopting an information literacy curriculum that is integrated across all curricular areas and involving parents and the community in the change process. Change that is evolutionary is much more likely to be lasting than unsupported change mandated from above. Therefore, changing slowly and seeking buy-in from all players in the process is very important.

REFERENCES

Note: All Web addresses accessed December 21, 2001.

AASL and AECT. (1998). *Information power: Building partnerships for learning.* Chicago: American Library Association.

Dalbotten, Mary S. (1998). Inquiry in the national content standards. In Daniel Callison, Joy H. McGregor, and Ruth V. Small (Eds.), *Instructional intervention for information use* (pp. 30–49). San Jose, CA: Hi Willow Research and Publishing.

Donham, J. (1998). Assessment of information processes and products. [Brochure]. McHenry, IL: Follett Software.

HyperStudio®. (2001). Knowledge Adventure.

Kagan, Spencer (1994). *Cooperative learning*. San Clemente, CA: Kagan Cooperative Learning.

McGregor, Joy H. (Ed.). (1999). How do we learn? In Barbara K. Stripling (Ed.), *Learning and libraries in an information age* (pp. 25–53). Englewood, CO: Libraries Unlimited.

Pappas, M. L. (1998). Designing authentic learning. *School Library Media Activities Monthly, 14* (6), 29–31, 42.

Pappas, M. L. (1999a). Changing learning and libraries in schools. *School Library Media Activities Monthly, 15* (1), 26–29, 32.

Pappas, M. L. (1999b). Learning communities. *School Library Media Activities Monthly, 15* (7), 30–32.

Pappas, M. L. (2000). Managing the inquiry learning environment. *School Library Media Activities Monthly, 16* (7), 27–30, 36.

PowerPoint®. (2001). Microsoft.

Rankin, V. (1999). *The thoughtful researcher: Teaching the research process to middle school students*. Englewood, CO: Libraries Unlimited.

Sheingold, Karen. (1987). Keeping children's knowledge alive through inquiry. *School Library Media Quarterly, 15* (2), 80–85.

SIRS Researcher®. Boca Raton, FL: SIRS. [Online]. Available: http://www.sirs.com /products/rfeatures.htm

WEB RESOURCES

Note: All Web addresses accessed December 21, 2001.

American Memory. (2001). Library of Congress. [Online]. Available: http://lcweb2 .loc.gov/ammem/

Electric Library. (2001). *Infonautics*. [Online]. Available: http://ask.elibrary.com/

NCPublic Schools.org. (n.d.). North Carolina Department of Public Instruction. [Online]. Available: http://www.dpi.state.nc.us/curriculum/information/ resources.html#TOP

Getting Started with Pathways

This chapter is about using Pathways to Knowledge with students who have little or no experience with inquiry learning. Classroom teachers and library media specialists often ask, "How do I get started?" "Where do I begin?" We provide some strategies and ideas that focus on new and novice users. Another frequently asked question is, "What does it look like?" Two scenarios appear in this unit that illustrate the planning and collaboration necessary between classroom teachers and library media specialists to integrate a process model into lessons and units of study. One is an elementary unit on whales and the other is a high school unit on Native Americans. The planning guide for whales appears as Figure C.1 in Appendix C and the planning guide for Native Americans is Appendix D. Information literacy, collaboration, and an inquiry design process are also covered in this chapter.

WHY INQUIRY?

At this point, we ask ourselves, How do we help you get started? What do you need to know in the early stages of using process and inquiry? We know you need to collaborate (teacher and library media specialist), that you need a plan before you start the unit, and that there are some important design characteristics that should be a part of your unit plan. We wrote the scenarios to show you how planning might happen. We developed the unit plans on whales and Native Americans to show you how each of the units might look as a plan. We encourage you to look these over for ideas that might help you get started. But the most important elements in getting started are excitement and enthusiasm, and we want to kindle those responses in you before we move into the mechanics of planning and designing.

We described in the Introduction how the fourth-grade students at Rosenwald–Dunbar Elementary School (RDES) in Nicholasville, Kentucky, became so enthusiastic about their inquiry project on mountaintop removal at Black Mountain that they were a significant voice in persuading Kentucky lawmakers to stop that action. During the time when students were engaged in this unit we were observers in the library media center at

RDES. As visitors, we were very uninformed about Black Mountain. The students' level of excitement was contagious. We observed students working in small groups, gathering information from a variety of sources, asking "good" questions, and recording information. We began questioning students, and their responses suggested that they had a good understanding of the various perspectives on the mountaintop removal problem. They could talk to us about the economic consequences of simply telling the coal mining companies to go away.

They understood why people who lived in the Black Mountain region might be reluctant to speak out against the coal mining companies on ecological issues. We read the thoughtful stories and poems they wrote. We also saw the unit plan their teacher developed, carefully crafted to cover the required learning outcomes from the Kentucky learning standards. She used the Black Mountain problem as content while she covered the fourth-grade outcomes in language arts, science, reading, math, and social studies. It was also apparent that these students had much experience as inquiry learners. They were learning to be responsible citizens in their community. They were also learning how to be lifelong learners.

We realize that this was a dream unit that was dropped in Sandy Adams's lap, but she and Barbara Greenlief picked up that ball and ran with it. All instructional units will not—cannot—be this compelling. But this is a vision that shows the exciting possibilities with inquiry learning. So, let's get started.

SCENARIO 3.1

Whales

SETTING THE STAGE: After returning from a conference, a teacher and library media specialist decide to collaboratively teach a unit on whales.

"When I did this unit last year, each student researched a type of whale and wrote a short report that included a picture of the whale, vital statistics, habitat, and endangered status. The reports were all created in a basic word processor using a consistent format. When they were finished, a couple of my volunteers put all of their reports together into a class book about whales. Each student got a copy of the book and a copy was donated to the library media center. I thought it was a good unit, but after we attended the conference last week I can see that it was knowledge-based, with little emphasis on critical thinking."

Anne Thomas, fifth-grade teacher, was talking with Sara Hancock, the school library media specialist. Anne and Sara had attended a session on information literacy and a process model, Pathways to Knowledge. They talked after the conference and decided they wanted to work together on a unit, using the Pathways model to help students become more information literate.

"How should we begin?" asked Anne. "The speaker talked about look-up assignments and changing these to be more of an inquiry project. I thought I might put more emphasis on whale migration and the endangered status."

"That's a good idea," said Sara.

"The speaker gave us an example of a planning guide [see Figure 3.2]. I think we should use it. Perhaps it will help us with our planning process," said Anne.

Anne and Sara began to use the planning guide as a framework for their planning process. They found the goals from their state learning standards in science and developed essential questions about whales to reflect those concepts. The English/language arts standards provided the goals for the research part of their unit.

Their next step was to decide how to use the Pathways model with students who had no previous experience with the process.

"Well," said Sara, "our choices include presenting the entire model or selecting some strategies from each stage, then using modeling and teacher direction to move them through the process this first time."

"I think if we show students the model as we begin the unit they will be overwhelmed," said Anne.

"I agree," said Sara. "I think we should select some strategies from each stage. I picked up a copy of the Pathways model that is blank except for the stages across the top. This would be a useful organizer to help students see where they will use specific strategies."

"That's a great idea," said Anne. "That will help them visualize their process, and we can use the organizer periodically throughout the unit to bring them back to a discussion of how their process matches what they actually did. Then we can use some writing prompts to engage students in thinking about how those strategies worked for them. When we finish the unit, we could show them the model with only the strategies we used in this unit. That way they can see the relationship of these strategies to the holistic process."

Sara and Anne decided to concentrate on the strategies of brainstorming, defining the question, using subject trees and the catalog, using a Favorites file to access Web sites, organizing and evaluating information, creating oceanic murals to show whale habitats and migration, and self-evaluation.

As they planned together they made decisions about who would teach various parts of the unit. They wanted to work as a team. They decided to use a clip from the video, In the Company of Whales, then involve the students in a discussion of the question, "What did you see in this video that arouses your curiosity?"

"I think this video and discussion will be a good engagement activity," said Sara. "We can encourage their questions, which is a good way to lead into a brainstorming session in Presearch."

At this point, Anne said, "I just had a great idea. I don't think my students know how to brainstorm. We could do some role playing for them to model how brainstorming actually works."

"I like that," said Sara. "Perhaps we should use a different topic so they can still proceed with a brainstorming activity on whales when we are finished."

The role-playing idea was incorporated into their instructional strategies. Next, they talked about the time students would need for research in the LMC. Sara knew the students had received instruction on using the catalog, but she would need to provide instruction on using subject trees like Yahooligans and KidsClick! Sara volunteered to find a selection of Web sites about whales and save them in a Favorites file. They worked together to decide on several graphic organizers that would help students organize their information. Anne had taught note taking earlier in the year, but she knew a review would be needed.

"I think we should use the space just outside the LMC for their murals," said Sara. "That will allow all the other students to view their work."

Anne and Sara set up a schedule for the unit, knowing they would have to be somewhat flexible as students began to gather and use their information. They remembered the conference speaker saying that inquiry can be messy and is often recursive. They also set up a couple of meeting times during the unit to assess progress.

When the unit was completed, they met to evaluate the unit. They wanted to use the evaluation to revise their unit.

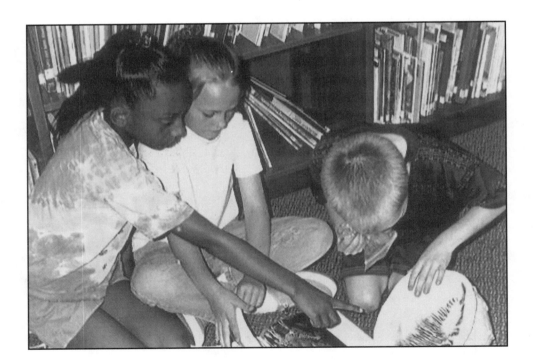

SCENARIO 3.2

Native Americans

SETTING THE STAGE: An English teacher and a library media specialist combine the writing process and the Pathways model as they plan a unit on stereotyping of Native Americans.

Mike Larson, high school English teacher, and Mindy Saechao, library media specialist, are talking about the commonalities between the writing process used by the English department and the Pathways model. They eat lunch at the same time each day, and they have been debating this topic for some time. "Certainly there are some similarities," Mike said, "but I'm not convinced students need another model. Our writing process works just fine."

"Then show me where gathering information is addressed in that process," said Mindy. "I think you will be surprised at how much more efficient your students will be if they use both models together. I think we should give it a try. We'll never know unless we do that."

"Okay, I'll try it," said Mike. "But won't we need extra time in the unit to teach about the Pathways model?"

"Most of your students have had at least a one-time experience with the Pathways model," said Mindy. "Ralph Recofsky used it in a social studies research project."

"Well, I think this might have merit in the longer class periods now that we are using a block schedule. We have a unit coming up next month that might work out well. We are going to study the stereotypes of Native Americans and then write a short story, a personal diary, or a magazine article."

The next week Mike and Mindy sat down to actually plan their unit. Mindy pulled out a copy of the planning guide. Together they began to fill it out. Mike had the state standards that would apply for both English and social studies. Mindy pointed to the standards in both English and social studies that related to information literacy.

"The seventh-grade art curriculum has a focus on Native Americans," said Mike. "Students created murals to depict daily life in Native American villages. That was a rather surface level approach, so I want this unit to really engage students in critical thinking."

"I've been doing some research in the media center on stereotypes," said Mindy. "I think we will have the resources students need. I've also checked on the Web and at the public library."

As they plotted out the schedule of events, Mindy showed Mike how she could integrate information literacy by using the Pathways model. Mindy also talked about inquiry learning and the importance of engagement and questioning.

"Both of those fit with the writing process," said Mike. "So, we should set up an activity early in the unit to really pique their interest and set the questioning mode in place. I like that. It really reflects what we try to do in Prewriting. We do a lot of brainstorming activities in Prewriting."

"Since students have had another experience with the Pathways model, I propose we show them the model right after the engagement activity. We can talk about the stages, point out the strategies we plan to focus on, and tell them that we want them to keep a journal about the process they follow throughout the unit. That journal will give us documentation to use for assessment of process at various stages," said Mindy.

"Good idea," said Mike. "I have used journals in the past, so students have some experience with them. We will have to use some writing prompts, however, to be sure they stay focused on this process."

"I've been investigating a software program called Inspiration®," said Mindy. "It is a graphics program that enables the creation of graphic organizers, including webs and mind maps. I would be willing to teach the students to use this software, and we could get students to create mind maps. It would also be useful as students are getting ready to write and in organizing their outline. Inspiration has a function that moves a web or mind map into outline format."

"Hey, that's great," said Mike.

"I will need to review using a **T** chart for note taking and the format for bibliographic citations," he added.

"Have you seen the Web site called NoodleTools?" asked Mindy.

"No," said Mike. "Tell me about it."

"There are several features in the site," Mindy explained. "One is called NoodleBib; it allows students to create a bibliography within a format of their choosing and it stores their bibliography on the Web until they are ready to use it in a paper or project. I can easily show them how to use it and add it to our Favorites file so they can find it."

"Students should have no problems finding information about the stereotyping of Native Americans," said Mike.

"I agree that there is lots of information available," said Mindy. "Their challenge will be in evaluating the information to avoid biases and organizing lots of information. I would like to be sure they start their searching with an effective focus, which ties into your Prewriting. They need well-developed research questions and then a little exercise in identifying keywords for their searches. Too often students want to just sit down at the computer and start in with a search engine. They get a huge hit list and take the first ten, which often have no relevance to their actual research project."

"Maybe we could team teach a lesson on Prewriting and Presearch combined," Mike suggested.

"I would really like to do that," Mindy responded.

As Mindy and Mike continued to plan, they decided that Mindy would create a Favorites file of Web sites about Native Americans. She would hold a brainstorming session with students to help them identify possible resources both in the school library and in the community. She also planned to hold several voluntary refresher sessions on search engines for those who might need a review.

Mike and Mindy planned the times that students would need to be in the library media center and/or the computer lab. Mike scheduled the time to review the other stages of the writing process. They decided that there was a correlation between the Drafting and Responding & Revising stages of the writing process with the Interpretation stage of Pathways. They talked about ways to engage students in the strategies of "compare" and "synthesize" that are on the Pathways model. Mindy pointed out that the Inspiration software program (version 6.0) has templates that show many different types of graphic organizers. She suggested they use the "Language Arts—Comparison" template to help students with organization of their information. Mindy said she wanted to be involved with reading student journals periodically because it would help her know how they were understanding the Pathways model process.

They decided they would hold short meetings during the unit on an unscheduled basis. They also talked about using e-mail to help with communication about immediate problems or concerns.

When the unit was concluded they met to look over projects, journals, and their own reflections about the unit. They evaluated the unit in terms of instructional and design effectiveness. They also evaluated the process they used to plan the unit.

PATHWAYS AND THE
INFORMATION LITERACY STANDARDS

The notion that another part of literacy is the ability to find and use information is not new. The American Library Association Presidential Committee on Information Literacy explored this concept and stated, "to be information literate, a person must be able to recognize when information is needed and have the ability to locate, evaluate, and use effectively the needed information" (1989, p. 1).

In 1998 the profession launched the *Information Literacy Standards for Student Learning* (ILS) (AASL and AECT). This document provides school library media specialists with a formal curriculum for the library media program. The standards stress that information literacy should be taught as a process and integrated within the context of the school curriculum.

The explosion of information-rich technologies has accelerated the need for an information literate population. We have become a knowledge-based society, and our students must be prepared to operate in that world when they become adults. They must be prepared to gather information, organize and evaluate enormous amounts of information to form new understandings, and use this new knowledge to make decisions and solve problems.

This is a time when many changes are occurring in education. Standardized testing and an emphasis on national and state standards are sweeping the country. Loud voices are promoting accountability in schooling. "The new standards [ILS] . . . come at a propitious juncture when major curriculum areas are redefining their national standards (NCTE, IRA, NCSS, NSTA, NCTM) and stressing thinking processes as integral to learning. Beyond concepts and skills to be mastered, these standards address methods of investigating and reasoning, means of communication, and notions of context" (Harada and Tepe, 1998, p. 9). The *Information Literacy Standards* include an emphasis on critical thinking and problem solving, which are an expanding focus in national standards and testing.

The Scans 2000 Workplace Know-how Competencies were developed by a group of business, labor, government, and education leaders. Among these competencies is one on information: "Effective workers can productively use information. They can acquire and evaluate data, organize and maintain files, interpret and communicate, and use computers to process information" (SCANS, 2000). SCANS 2000 also emphasizes the importance of lifelong learning for workers in the twenty-first century. "Information literacy—the ability to find and use information—is the keystone of lifelong learning" (AASL and AECT, 1998, p. 1).

Librarians have taught library skills for many years. When librarians taught library skills, students learned to use the catalog, an encyclopedia, periodical indexes, or the Dewey Decimal System, often with no curriculum connection. How are the *Information Literacy Standards* different? Information literacy is taught within the context of the curriculum and presented as a process rather than disparate parts with no connections. Today, within the context of information literacy, library media specialists guide students toward identifying an information need, developing questions focused on that need, using a variety of resources based on the research questions, evaluating information, and so forth. This does not mean that there is no need to know how to use a catalog or an encyclopedia. Rather, within the framework of

process, students learn that there are tools for locating information, and the catalog is one of many such tools.

Pathways to Knowledge is an information process model with many connections to the *Information Literacy Standards*. Table 3.1, page 50, shows the nine *Information Literacy Standards* and a selection of stages and strategies from the Pathways model that correlate with each standard. The *Information Literacy Standards* are divided into three broad categories: Information Literacy, Independent Learning, and Social Responsibility. Each standard includes indicators followed by levels of proficiency (Basic, Proficient, and Exemplary). Each standard also includes a selection of examples that show how the standards might be used within the context of a lesson or unit. There is also a sampling of content-area standards that correlate with the *Information Literacy Standards*. For a more in-depth look at the standards, teachers and library media specialists are encouraged to examine the complete documents.

State departments of education and school districts have developed their own information literacy standards. In some cases they have developed documents that integrate the information literacy concepts into content area standards. For example, the *Illinois Learning Standards* integrated information literacy into the *Research Goal* of the *English/ Language Arts Standards* (2001). Other states have created separate standards documents for information literacy. The *North Carolina Standard Course of Study* includes a separate set of standards for *Information Skills* (1999/2000). We encourage you to find out about the information literacy standards for your state.

COLLABORATION

The idea of collaboration is not new. Educators have long been promoting collaboration among teachers (e.g., classroom, special, and library media) as a means to make learning more authentic and interdisciplinary. However, most teachers' early learning experiences, teacher education courses, and teaching experience focused on the teacher as an independent person who had autonomy within the classroom. For many educators, collaboration is a new experience, one regarded with some suspicion and trepidation. Teachers are accustomed to being independent operators in their own classrooms, so making the move to being a team player seems like more work with little personal benefit. Library media specialists and teachers do engage in collaboration in many schools today, but this is often a lesser, more service-oriented form of collaboration rather than the higher level required for inquiry learning. To effectively engage in inquiry learning, teachers and library media specialists must move beyond the service role.

What Is Collaboration?

Collaboration is a teaming or partnership between two or more professional educators to provide learning experiences for students. Within the context of the library media program and the information literacy standards, collaboration enables the library media specialist and classroom teachers to integrate information literacy into content areas of the curriculum. When library media specialists and teachers collaborate at a higher level, they share responsibilities for designing and conducting a unit of study.

Table 3.1. Pathways to Knowledge® and *Information Literacy*

Pathways to Knowledge® and *Information Literacy*

Information Literacy Standards for Student Learning

Information Literacy			Independent Learning			Social Responsibility		
Standard 1	**Standard 2**	**Standard 3**	**Standard 4**	**Standard 5**	**Standard 6**	**Standard 7**	**Standard 8**	**Standard 9**
"The student who is information literate accesses information efficiently and effectively" (p. 8).	"The student who is information literate evaluates information critically and competently" (p. 8).	"The student who is information literate uses information accurately and creatively" (p. 8).	"The student who is an independent learner is information literate and pursues information related to personal interests" (p. 8).	"The student who is an independent learner is information literate and appreciates literature and other creative expressions of information" (p. 8).	"The student who is an independent learner is information literate and strives for excellence in information seeking and knowledge generation" (p. 9).	"The student who contributes positively to the learning community and to society is information literate and recognizes the importance of information to a democratic society" (p. 9).	"The student who contributes positively to the learning community and to society is information literate and practices ethical behavior in regard to information and information technology" (p. 9).	"The student who contributes positively to the learning community and to society is information literate and participates effectively in groups to pursue and generate information" (p. 9).

Pathways to Knowledge

Pathways strategies may appear under more than one Information Literacy Standard, although an attempt has been made here to limit repetition. Be aware that overlap is frequent between the strategies and the standards.

Standard 1	Standard 2	Standard 3	Standard 4	Standard 5	Standard 6	Standard 7	Standard 8	Standard 9
Presearch Define question/need Relate to prior knowledge Develop an overview Explore relationships Search Identify information providers Select information resources and tools Seek relevant information Specific search strategies Overall Evaluate Reflect	Search Determine relevancy (fact or fiction, accuracy, currency, primary and secondary sources) Interpretation Filter (point of view, bias, relevancy) Note: *Using Interpretation strategies (e.g., organize, classify, analyze, integrate concepts) often cause searchers to go back to Presearch and/or Search in a recursive manner.* Overall Appreciate Evaluate Reflect	Interpretation Synthesize Determine themes, patterns, trends Communication Organize information Apply information Share new knowledge Answer a question Satisfy a need Solve a problem Choose appropriate communication format Evaluate format selection Overall Evaluate Reflect	Appreciation Viewing Sensing Listening Reading Enjoyment Curiosity Evaluation Evaluate end product	Appreciation Viewing Sensing Listening Reading Enjoyment Curiosity Interpretation Respect intellectual property Communication Share new knowledge Overall Evaluate Reflect	Evaluation Check for effective communication of new knowledge Assess/reassess personal information-seeking process Evaluate and redefine the question Evaluate end product Overall Appreciate Reflect	Search Select information resources and tools Interpretation Filter (point of view, bias, relevancy) Communication Respect intellectual property Overall Appreciate Evaluate Reflect	Interpretation Practice responsible, ethical use of information Communication Respect intellectual property Overall Appreciate Evaluate Reflect	Note: *This standard is fostered within a student-centered learning environment that is equally important for the application of Pathways.* Overall Many Pathways strategies apply

The teacher brings extensive knowledge of the subject or discipline to which the unit is related. He also has significant knowledge of his students, their learning styles, and their prior knowledge. The library media specialist also brings expertise into this partnership. As a teacher, she understands curriculum design, learning theory, and information literacy. She contributes significant knowledge about the resources that provide the information students need to successfully write papers, create projects, solve authentic problems, and investigate the issues of their world.

Information technology has exploded into learning and libraries and will be a significant part of the world our students will inherit as adults. School library media specialists bring their knowledge of and skill with information technology into collaborative partnerships as well.

At the higher levels of collaboration, there is a blending in the roles of classroom teacher and library media specialist. They truly become partners, with each developing a comfort level with the other's more traditional role. Sharon Coatney is the library media specialist in Oak Hill Elementary School (Overland Park, Kansas). Sharon and the teachers in her school are an excellent example of a blending of roles. The learning program at Oak Hill is almost totally inquiry based. The library media center is truly the learning laboratory of the school. Students use this media center throughout the day, and their teachers coach and tutor their students with skills that often were traditionally taught by a library media specialist. Sharon can often be found in classrooms, either teaching information literacy skills or a more content-oriented lesson. In many ways she has become a coordinator for inquiry learning across the curriculum.

David Loertscher (1999) has written about the difference between support and intervention as these relate to collaboration. Distinguishing between these two concepts is important because it underscores the differences that are reflected in the behavior of library media specialists as they work with teachers. Many library media specialists provide resources to support learning experiences of students. They pull classroom sets and send them down the hall or put them on a cart to be used in the media center. The notion of support, or service, fits well in the traditional model, where the classroom teacher and textbooks are the primary source of information. Resources from the school library are supplemental; nice to have but not absolutely necessary. Support is more a cooperative role for a library media specialist than it is collaboration. Intervention is at the opposite end of the continuum from support. As Loertscher (1999) describes:

> [L]ibrary media specialists understand that to have a greater impact on teaching and learning they must begin to move along the continuum toward intervention. They begin by giving advice, providing alternatives, and making suggestions and recommendations. They continue by asking for reconsiderations of a request or suggesting more powerful strategies/technologies to meet a problem. At some point along the scale they evolve from servant to trusted advisor and, finally to partner. (p. 70)

For many, this level of collaboration is a new concept, and the question always is, "What does it look like?" Loertscher astutely places the concepts of support and intervention on a continuum, which is very real. It takes time and experience for library media specialists and teachers to learn to collaborate at the intervention level. There is a video entitled *Collaboration: Searching as a Process* (1997) that illustrates collaboration between library media specialists and teachers in various school settings. The *Collaboration* video presents several examples of collaboration at the intervention level, giving those who want to move in that direction a goal for which to strive.

Collaboration between library media specialists and teachers requires a collaborative culture brought about through effective communication, the availability of time, and a trusting relationship between teachers and the library media specialist (*Collaboration*, 1997). In Scenario 3.2, Mike (English teacher) and Mindy (LMS) were holding a friendly lunchtime debate about combining the writing process with the Pathways model when students had a writing assignment. Eventually, Mike conceded and agreed to work with Mindy on the Native American unit. As their planning process took shape, their conversation showed a positive level of trust between these two educators.

Finding time will always be a challenge in schools, but Mindy and Mike obviously found time to hold their planning meeting and to schedule several other short meetings as the unit progressed. Teachers usually have some type of preparation period, and these are never long enough. Finding a common planning time in a block schedule can be a challenge. Some time for planning, either a designated planning time during the school day or before and after school, is a critical element in the success of collaboration. Obviously, some communication must occur during a formal planning meeting. Because allocating time for meetings can be a challenge, teachers and library media specialists must be creative. Meetings during lunch or stand-up meetings can be used to cover a short agenda.

The other part of a collaborative culture is communication, among and between all members of the learning community. Trust depends on at least some minimal level of communication. For a collaborative culture to exist, the administration must be involved, and that involvement also requires communication. A principal in one of the inquiry-based schools we visited had an exciting philosophy. He believed that for inquiry learning to thrive in the school, his role was to remove all of the impediments so that teachers could instruct and students could learn.

Technology can be an effective medium to enable communication. An expanding number of teachers have a computer on their desks in the classroom. More often today these are laptops, purchased for them by the school system with an understanding that this form of technology is now an essential tool for teachers. Schools now have networks that connect classrooms, and these networks have Internet and intranet access. This means that teachers and library media specialists can communicate easily via e-mail, shortening the communication loop because there is no hunt-and-wait time.

Some educators have begun to use threaded discussion forums for communication. Software application programs are now available on school networks that enable protected discussion forums and also chat rooms. A growing number of Web authoring programs have features that allow Web authors to install protected forums and chats on school Web sites. Educational portals like *BigChalk*™ and *Lightspan* also offer these features with the concept of enabling communication within a learning community.

Discussion forums are asynchronous (i.e., not in real time), with a threaded discussion area that can be either public or private. This feature enables a conversation between educators that does not require their presence together in the same room. A private forum is only open to those individuals whose names have been selected for this specific forum.

This software can be made available from home through the Web, which would allow for conversations in the time away from school. In this type of discussion format, messages do not appear in users' mailboxes but instead are stored on the server that runs the portal software. Because the messages are threaded (connected together by topic), there is an obvious sequence to these messages that allows a user to look back over other related messages.

For example, suppose Mindy is working on her part of the lesson about using *Inspiration* to create a mind map, and she wants to be sure she includes a focus on some Pathways Presearch strategies and the Prewriting stage of the writing process. She can go into the school's Web site and click on the discussion area. The selection of the Native American unit takes her to their private discussion forum. She can type a quick message to Mike and then log off. Later in the day, she can check back in the discussion forum and find a response from Mike. Granted, this same discussion can take place in regular e-mail, but the threaded forum keeps messages easily available in a longitudinal organization.

Why Collaborate?

So, why collaborate? Well, probably the most important reason is that teaching information literacy skills separately and out of context does not work. This situation is much like the one a mathematics, writing, or reading teacher encounters. Students sometimes learn skills for writing a paper in language arts class but cannot apply those skills in science when a lab report is needed. Or students learn to add and subtract in math class but later in life they cannot balance their checkbooks. In the same way that these writing and math skills must relate to the authentic world, students should learn the information literacy process within the context of an actual research task. Even more important, students need to learn that gathering and using information can be used to solve a problem or make a decision whether or not it is related to a school assignment. When students leave the school environment and enter the working world as adults, they will need these skills.

Library media specialists are typically teachers because many states require teaching certification prior to acquiring a school library media certification. Curriculum designs are changing to a more constructivist approach to learning, and instructional practices have shifted away from large-group, teacher-directed learning to student-centered learning. In this environment, students work in small groups or individually on projects, and classroom management changes. Collaboration means there is another teacher and partner available (the library media specialist) to help plan the unit, instruct, coach or tutor students, and facilitate as students work in small groups. Changing curriculum designs may happen more slowly where state standards are based on rote memorization of facts instead of higher-level thinking.

INQUIRY DESIGN PROCESS

Designing a unit that is based on inquiry and incorporates both content standards and information literacy standards follows a process, which is illustrated in Figure 3.1.

Set the Stage

As the teacher and LMS begin the process of designing a unit, they typically start with several activities that set the stage for their unit. Often, they want to revise a unit or develop a new curricular concept. Sometimes a current topic of interest might pique the interest of the teacher or even students, and this fuels an idea for a new unit. In Scenario 3.1, Anne Thomas, a fifth-grade teacher, and Sara Hancock, the LMS, decide to revise a unit because they want to add a greater focus on critical thinking and a process model—Pathways.

When teachers either revise a unit or develop a new one, they often need to gather background knowledge from the teacher resources and/or spend some time in the library to determine the potential scope of the unit. At this point, as a collaborative partner, the library media specialist's expertise with available resources can be invaluable.

The instructional unit must follow district or state standards or goals. For example, in Scenario 3.2, the teacher, Mike, and the library media specialist, Mindy, who were working on a Native American unit, first went to the district's English curriculum for the appropriate goals and benchmarks. Mike and Mindy are teaching in a high school that just began to implement block scheduling. That type of schedule might allow a social studies teacher to participate in this teaming experience also, and that type of partnership is important today with the focus on interdisciplinary or integrated curriculum.

If you are interested in the English standards for your state or at the national level, the Web site *Developing Educational Standards* covers the state standards for all of the states. The examples provided in both the whales and Native American planning guides in Appendixes C and D use the Illinois Learning Standards. Illinois chose to integrate information literacy into the Research Goal of the English/language arts standards.

Figure 3.1. Inquiry Design Process.

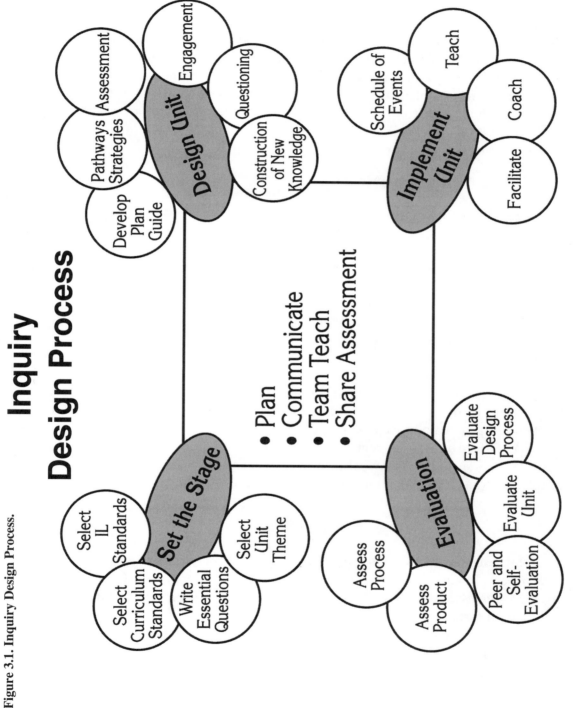

Inquiry
Design Process

- Plan
- Communicate
- Team Teach
- Share Assessment

Set the Stage
- Select IL Standards
- Select Curriculum Standards
- Write Essential Questions
- Select Unit Theme

Design Unit
- Assessment
- Pathways Strategies
- Develop Plan Guide
- Engagement
- Questioning
- Construction of New Knowledge

Implement Unit
- Schedule of Events
- Teach
- Coach
- Facilitate

Evaluation
- Assess Process
- Assess Product
- Peer and Self-Evaluation
- Evaluate Unit
- Evaluate Design Process

In this type of collaborative unit, it is not enough to establish only the content standards. Another part of the design is to decide on the information literacy standards or goals that are part of the school or state curriculum. The strategies of the Pathways model are then selected—those that need review and those that will require instruction. The students in Scenario 3.1 are fifth-grade students who have not previously used the Pathways model. Anne and Sara discussed the best way to introduce their students to the model. They also made decisions about the strategies they would focus on in this unit.

Their next step was to write several essential questions that provide a conceptual and big picture framework for the unit. An example of essential questions can be found in the whale planning guide (see Appendix C); some of those questions are included here:

- How do whales live?

- How do whales migrate?

- Why are whales endangered?

Essential questions establish a questioning atmosphere and demonstrate to students from the very beginning that questioning is an important part of the unit.

Contemporary curriculum developers often use essential questions or understandings as the framework or conceptual structure of a unit (Wiggins and McTighe, 1998; Jacobs, 1997; McKenzie, 2000). Essential questions shift the focus away from regurgitation of facts to higher-level thinking. For example, assignments that ask students to identify the causes of the American Civil War set up opportunities for plagiarism, but an essential question that asks, "How did the American Civil War change the lives of people today?" guarantees a much higher level of critical thinking. Another approach might be, "How is my life different today as a result of the American Civil War?" That answer would be difficult to find out on the Web.

Many school districts and some states still write curriculum based on behavioral objectives. These are usually more specific than conceptual goals or standards, but it is still possible to write essential questions to correlate with these objectives.

Design Unit

Unit design involves developing a planning guide, identifying the Pathways strategies to teach, setting up activities that foster student engagement and questioning, designing scaffolds that enable students to construct new knowledge, and the criteria and strategies for assessment and unit evaluation.

Unit Planning Guide

A planning guide is documentation of the unit theme, standards, and essential questions (or concepts), the instructional strategies, assessment, and schedule for the unit. An example is included in this chapter as Figure 3.2, pages 57–58. These planning guides can be long or short, but some basic elements should be included. The template will allow for expanding each section of the guide as the need for additional space grows.

Figure 3.2. Unit Planning Guide.

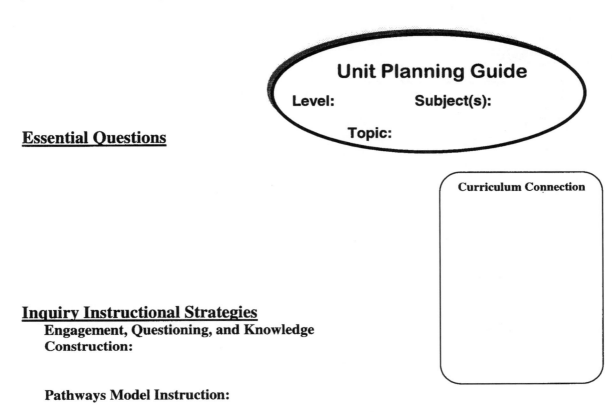

Essential Questions

Unit Planning Guide

Level: Subject(s):

Topic:

Curriculum Connection

Inquiry Instructional Strategies
Engagement, Questioning, and Knowledge
Construction:

Pathways Model Instruction:

Students are:

New Users	Novice Users	Proficient Users	Independent Users

Pathways model strategies to be taught in this unit:

Appreciation	Presearch	Search	Interpretation	Communication	Evaluation

Assessment
Criteria:

Strategies:

(Figure 3.2 continues on page 58.)

Figure 3.2—Continued

Unit Schedule

Date	Teacher	Library Media Specialist	Student

Collaboration Notes

Resources

Reproducible from *Pathways to Knowledge® and Inquiry Learning* by Marjorie L. Pappas and Ann E. Tepe (Libraries Unlimited, 2002).

In Scenario 3.1, Anne and Sara are meeting to plan a unit on whales. Because the class had no prior experience with a process model, Sara and Anne were carefully planning their strategy for the model introduction. Anne brought up the idea of a planning guide, and they agreed to use it for their unit. They followed the guide as they identified the standards for the unit and wrote essential questions. They decided to use a clip from a video to foster student engagement, with a follow-up discussion about things in the video that aroused student curiosity.

They decided to use a blank version of the Pathways model as a graphic organizer to help students visualize their planning process (see Figure A.3 in Appendix A). The graphic organizer might also be used as a log for students to record their process throughout a unit (see student sample, Figure C.2 in Appendix C). Their research plan could be recorded on the organizer in one color and the actual process in another color.

Questioning is an important part of inquiry learning. Students should be encouraged to question throughout the unit, and an environment of wonder should prevail. Students should know that their questions and ideas are valued. Questioning is a skill students must learn. Typically, they start by asking questions that are low level and to which there is a finite answer. For example, the question "Do birds fly" has a typical response of "Yes." A higher-level question might be, "Why do birds fly?" or "How do birds fly?" Rubrics can be useful strategies for teaching students how to question. Jamie McKenzie's *Questioning Toolkit* (1997) is an excellent resource for teaching about questioning.

Constructing new knowledge is also listed on the Unit Planning Guide under "Inquiry Instructional Strategies" because this is the last critical piece for students. Some thought should be given as to how this will work for students. Students construct new knowledge through reflective writing, journals, and using graphic organizers such as mind maps that help them see the big picture and the relationships between subsets of information. The students working on the Native American unit (see Appendix D) use mind maps to help them organize their information and to show how their information is related. They also use comparison charts to help them find patterns and trends in their information. David Hyerle's books, *Visual Tools for Constructing Knowledge* (1996) and *A Field Guide to Using Visual Tools* (2000), are excellent resources for graphic organizers to help students with constructing new knowledge. Inspiration software enables students to create a variety of graphic organizers that are useful for knowledge construction. Check out the template library of graphic organizers.

Another inquiry instructional strategy that requires some prior planning is the use of small group activities. Constructivist theory suggests that students construct new understandings through social interaction. This means planning activities that engage students in projects that require meaningful small group activities. Whenever possible, it is important for each small group to have a task that ultimately will reflect the outcome of the larger group (the class) task or project. For example, in the Native American unit, groups are gathering information about stereotyping of Native Americans as portrayed in a specific medium (e.g., film, fiction, nonfiction, paintings). The small groups constructed mind maps that showed the information they gathered. Toward the end of the unit, the class used an Inspiration template, "Language Arts—Comparison," as a strategy for combining all of their significant information and looking for trends or patterns.

Pathways Strategies

Because our goal in this chapter is to focus on getting started with a process model, this seems like a good place to address the issue of new or novice users of Pathways. The challenge that library media specialists and teachers face is that new users—those who have never used a process model before—can be from primary grades all the way up to senior high school students. They all need a basic understanding of process, but older students will come to this learning activity with skills and knowledge that a primary student would not have. It is fair to assume that the timetable for "new" high school users to learn to use Pathways might be shorter than the time required for elementary students.

The Unit Planning Guide (Figure 3.2) includes a table that focuses teachers and the library media specialist on the level of experience that students will have with regard to using the Pathways model. In the whale unit (see Appendix C) students are New Users, but in the Native American unit (see Appendix D) students are Novice Users. In Figure 3.3, the stages of Pathways are listed across the top. The bottom box gives teachers an opportunity to think about and post those Pathways strategies that will be taught during the implementation of the unit.

Figure 3.3 shows how Pathways strategies might be applied as students move from the status of New User to Independent User. There is some difference in this progression between students who are very young and those who are older. For example, the chart shows primary students as new users experiencing a brainstorming activity. As a contrast, the chart also shows high school students engaging in brainstorming. The high school students have not used Pathways before, but they do know how to brainstorm and use Inspiration software.

Library media specialists and teachers are encouraged to think about the level of their students' experience with Pathways and their prior knowledge of strategies but not process as they plan inquiry units. Also, if this section is regularly completed on the Unit Planning Guide, teachers and library media specialists will have a visual record of those strategies taught during units.

Assessment

Another part of the unit design is to develop the strategies and criteria the teacher and library media specialist will use to assess the outcome of the unit. Assessment should include students' ability to apply the process; that is, the stages and strategies of Pathways, and students' understanding of the content knowledge required to respond to the essential questions. Strategies often take the form of a project or authentic task as a means of assessing content knowledge. Strategies also include journals, graphic organizers, and prompted writing in the form of reflections to assess process. Criteria are the benchmarks against which those strategies will be measured.

Figure 3.3. Pathways User Levels.

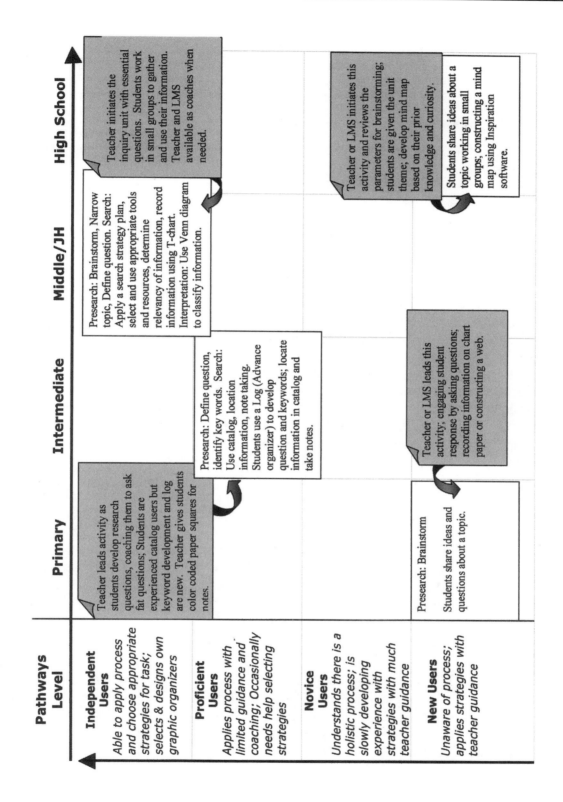

For example, the assessment criteria for stories or diaries about stereotyping of Native Americans (Scenario 3.2) might include historical accuracy and an understanding of perspective. Students wrote journals based on prompts posted by their teacher, Mike Larson. When the unit concluded, the library media specialist asked students to review their journals and write a reflection on the overall process. Some writing prompts to use at this point are:

♦ How did the research plan developed by your group affect the outcome of your research?

♦ How might you change the research plan when you have another research assignment?

Mike Larson asked students to use a T chart as a means of taking notes. Another strategy for assessing process is to ask students to highlight the parts of their T chart that demonstrate how they made a connection to prior knowledge.

Implement the Unit

Implementing the unit means following the Unit Planning Guide. The guide includes a rather detailed schedule of events, but it is important to remember that inquiry learning requires a flexible schedule. When the schedule was established, the teachers made decisions about instructing and/or facilitating specific parts of the unit. For example, in Scenario 3.2 Mike Larson, the high school English teacher, and Mindy Saechao, the elementary library media specialist, plan to use *Inspiration* when students brainstorm to construct mind maps.

Students had some previous experience with brainstorming but they had not used the *Inspiration* software program. They arranged for students to use the computer lab in the library media center, where *Inspiration* resides on the network. Mindy and Mike plan to jointly facilitate the mind mapping session, but Mindy will teach students to use *Inspiration*. As the teacher and LMS planned, they set up a tentative schedule showing what both Mindy and Mike would be doing throughout the unit. There is also a column to show what students would be doing.

Evaluation

When the unit is completed, all of the teachers involved in the unit should meet to evaluate the process they followed throughout the unit. For example, should there be additional members of the teaching team? How did the brainstorming session work with students using *Inspiration*? Were there enough resources for students to use as they gathered information?

REFERENCES

Note: All Web addresses accessed December 21, 2001.

AASL and AECT. (1998). *Information literacy standards for student learning.* Chicago: American Library Association.

Abilock, D., and D. Abilock. (1999–2001). *NoodleTools.* [Online]. Available: http://www.noodletools.com/
(Tools include NoodleBib and NoodleQuest.)

American Library Association Presidential Committee on Information Literacy. (1989). *Final Report.* Chicago: American Library Association.

Collaboration: Searching as a process. (1997). [Video]. Know It All series. Lincoln, NE: Great Plains National.

Harada, V., and A. Tepe. (1998). Pathways to Knowledge. *Teacher Librarian*, 26 (2), 9–15.

Hyerle, D. (1996). *Visual tools for constructing knowledge.* Alexandria, VA: Association for Supervision and Curriculum Development.

Hyerle, D. (2000). *A field guide to using visual tools.* Alexandria, VA: Association for Supervision and Curriculum Development.

Inspiration® (version 6.0). (1988–1999). Inspiration Software.

Jacobs, H. H. (1997). *Mapping the big picture.* Alexandria, VA: Association for Supervision and Curriculum Development.

Loertscher, D. V. (1999). (2d ed.). *Taxonomies of the school library media program.* San Jose, CA: Hi Willow Research and Publishing.

McKenzie, J. (2000). *Beyond technology: Questioning, research, and the information literate school.* Bellingham, WA: FNO Press.

Wiggins, G., and J. McTighe. (1998). *Understanding by design.* Alexandria, VA: Association for Supervision and Curriculum Development.

WEB RESOURCES

Note: All Web addresses accessed December 21, 2001.

Big Chalk™. (2001). [Online]. Available: http://schools.bigchalk.com/portal

Developing Educational Standards. (2000). {Online] Maintained by Charles Hill. Wappingers Central School District. (NY). http://edstandards.org/standards.html

Illinois Learning Standards. English/Language Arts Standards. Research Goal. (1997). Illinois State Board of Education. [Online]. Available: http://www.isbe.state.il.us /ils/english/english.html

International Reading Association. (IRA). (1996–2001). [Online] Available: http://www.reading.org/

Lightspan. (2000). [Online]. Available: http://www.lightspan.com/

McKenzie, Jamie. (1997). *Questioning toolkit.* [Online]. Available: http://questioning.org/Q7/toolkit.html

National Council of Teachers of English. NCTE. (2001). [Online]. Available: http://www.ncte.org/

National Council for the Social Studies. NCSS. (2001). [Online]. Available: http://www.ncss.org/

National Science Teachers Association. NSTA. (n.d.). [Online]. Available: http://www.nsta.org/

National Council of Teachers of Mathematics. NCTM. (n.d.). [Online]. Available: http://www.nctm.org/

North Carolina standard course of study: Information skills. (1999/2000). [Online]. Available: http://www.dpi.state.nc.us/curriculum/

SCANS 2000: The workforce skills website. (2001). Johns Hopkins University. [Online]. Available: http://www.scans.jhu.edu/NS/HTML/Index.htm

Pathways and the Tools of Technology

Over the past ten years, the presence of technology has exploded into schools. Students and teachers have access to extensive, full-text periodical and magazine databases often available on statewide virtual libraries. Tool software enables students to compose their assignments electronically and easily revise their work. Graphic tools allow students to brainstorm ideas, organize and analyze information, and communicate new understandings in a visual mode that enables them to look at relationships and construct solutions to real-world problems.

The Internet has opened a portal to the world for students as they study in classrooms, in libraries, or at home. Students can access the *Library of Congress*, explore the *British Museum's* online tour, actively engage in scientific research by sharing and manipulating data with students located around the world, question experts like NASA astronauts, and take classes through online schools. In a virtual sense, the walls of the school—and the library media center—have crumbled. Schooling can now occur anywhere and anytime.

This chapter explores the possibilities for using technology resources and tools with the Pathways stages and strategies. Although print resources will be with us for many years, today's children will inherit a technology- and information-rich world that will be vastly different from the world of their parents and grandparents. Information glut will be commonplace, so students' ability to apply a process to achieve their information needs must become second nature. They will need to be experts at selecting and using electronic tools and sophisticated resources. If this is to happen, they must learn to use these tools now in their formative years. This chapter shows how electronic resources and tools can enable and enhance the information-seeking process.

This chapter contains a great deal of information. We suggest you read it through once and then go back to mark sections you know you will want to use later as a reference.

APPRECIATION

The Appreciation stage of the Pathways model reflects the emphasis placed on appreciation by the *Information Literacy Standards for Student Learning* (AASL and AECT, 1998). Both the model and the standards recognize the importance of reading but also reflect the significance of appreciating and developing creative forms of expression in many different formats. Appreciation also includes a focus on discovery and exploration. Curiosity is a vital part of critical thinking and should be nurtured and developed within an inquiry learning environment. Many educators place great emphasis today on the importance of lifelong learning. Curiosity and questioning are skills that adults need to be lifelong learners.

There are many resources on the Web that teachers and students can use to foster literary appreciation. We highlight some of those in this section.

Literary Appreciation

Literary appreciation has been an integral part of the library media program and should not cease with the appearance of technology resources in the library media center. There are many resources to enhance literary appreciation using technology, with the understanding that the technology resource does not replace the book but rather becomes a value-added piece. This section focuses on some examples of literary Web resources.

Children and young adults have always enjoyed the opportunity to meet their favorite authors. Technology allows students to learn more about authors by visiting their Web sites. At *The Author Corner* students can find links to many author Web sites. *The Reading Corner* includes links for award books (e.g., Newbery, Caldecott, and state award books) and lists books for young adults. The *Coretta Scott King Award* books are listed on an ALA Web page. Authors such as Gary Paulson, Marc Brown, and Jan Brett have Web sites that showcase their books and provide information about the authors. *The Official Eric Carle Web* site has a Caterpillar Exchange Bulletin Board where teachers and students can post creative ways they are using Carle's books. The Guestbook section allows students to ask Eric Carle questions. *Virginia Hamilton's Web* site has a place where students can ask her questions.

Teachers and library media specialists are always looking for strategies to encourage students to read. *The 100 Favorite Children's Books* Web site includes an exciting list of book titles with annotations. *"On-Lion" for Kids* encourages children to read and pursue their literary interests on the Web. Both of these webs are maintained by the New York Public Library. The *Young Adult Literature* Web site focuses on the reading interests of older students.

Media Appreciation

Appreciation is more than being a consumer. What about other creative forms of expression? There are Web sites that encourage student writing and publish their products on the Web. *Kids' Space* is an international exhibit for stories and pictures from young writers and artists.

Virtual museums allow students to visit facilities around the world and enjoy art that reflects diverse cultures. For example, the *Louvre Museum* in France and the *National Gallery of Art* in Washington, D.C., have Web sites. Both of these museums have virtual tours. The *Virtual Library Museum Pages* is a comprehensive international list of virtual museums, galleries, and libraries.

Science museums have taken on a new dimension in the virtual world. They still maintain the fascinating exhibits within the physical space of the museum, but the virtual museum now reaches many more people. The *Exploratorium* is a museum that strives to help people develop their sense of curiosity. The *Franklin Institute Online* has a similar mission. Franklin's Forecast allows students the opportunity to be weather scientists. They can make a weather station or be weather watchers. Many of the online activities within the *Franklin Institute Online* have an inquiry focus. For example, the description of the Living Things area states: "This unit of study will stimulate critical thinking. . . . Hands-on science with inquiry-based facilitation provides motivation for learning."

Children's museums have become popular today. *The Virtual Museum for Children* includes a comprehensive list of children's museums. *The Children's Museum of Indianapolis* has some great graphics. Selecting Fun Online and Geo Mysteries takes a visitor to Rex the Dino Detective. Rex asks questions about geological exhibits and even shows an erupting volcano.

Curiosity and Questioning

Students who engage in inquiry are encouraged to question. We ask students, "What do you wonder about?" "What are you curious about?" Young children are very curious; they are like sponges. Our challenge as educators is to keep that curiosity alive and growing. There are some exciting Web sites with that purpose. One is *Dragonfly*. The *Dragonfly* home page opens with a picture of two children fishing in a pond. Many parts of this scene have links, and students are encouraged to click on the links that interest them. The Web site has many opportunities for active learning, such as sections on baseball in space, hide and seek, and earth sounds.

There are search engines that use natural language to encourage students to ask questions as their search phrase. Both *Ask Jeeves* and *Ask Jeeves for Kids* operate in this manner. The software even returns the hit list based on variations of the original question.

PRESEARCH

The primary function of the Presearch stage is to establish a focus for the search. Using Presearch strategies, students can develop an overview of their topic or explore the relationships between topics. Before they move on into the Search stage, students should develop a research question.

General Resources

Developing an overview of a topic requires that students gather some background information from general resources. There are many resources on the Web that provide general information to help students gain an understanding of the scope of their topic.

Often, students need to build some background information before they can examine the relationships between those subtopics related to the broader topic. Librarians or skilled information specialists typically use an encyclopedia or a general resource that covers the broad scope of a subject in shallow depth to gather general background information before proceeding with a more in-depth search. There are many general resources on the Web that students can use to gather background information. For example, *Encarta Encyclopedia* includes encyclopedia articles, an atlas, and the *World English Dictionary*. The search function of *Encarta* uses natural language. Students can enter a question in the search box, and the software returns a response that includes a selection of articles in the encyclopedia and Web sites.

Explore is one of the strategies available in the Pathways Search stage. Explore has great relevance in Presearch because it is a strategy that enables students to peruse a variety of Web sites as they hyperlink in a serendipitous manner, making connections to their prior knowledge and building background knowledge. For example, students studying animals might start with a visit to *eNature.com*, a Web site that provides general information on various types of animals. As they read about animals that interest them, they might decide that they are curious about habitats and click on that link.

A virtual library is a collection of Web resources that have been selected using specific criteria. These Web sites offer learners many opportunities to pursue the Explore strategy of Pathways. An example of a virtual library is the *Awesome Library,* which has many resources that provide information on different topics. Students who are just curious about a variety of topics might explore and discover new information on this site. The *New York Times* has a Web page entitled *Navigator* that was originally developed for their journalists to help them use the Web. They have made this page public, and it has many interesting sites that students could explore.

Presearch Tools

The Web also has sites that provide tools for students and teachers to use with Presearch strategies. One is *Filamentality,* which teachers or students can use to develop treasure hunts that send students to specified Web sites in response to an established set of questions. At an early stage of a project or research unit, teachers can establish a treasure hunt using general resources on the Web. *Filamentality* provides templates that guide a user through the treasure hunt development process, which typically consists of selecting a variety of Web sites around a topic and writing a question relevant to the content on each of the sites.

Graphic organizers are important tools for Presearch strategies. Graphic organizers enable students to visualize the relationships between topics or ideas and use that as a catalyst for connecting ideas and establishing relationships. If you have not used webs for brainstorming with students, check out David Hyerle's books (1996, 2000). Hyerle understands the significance of the visual dimension as a tool that fuels thinking. He writes about visual fluency and suggests that brainstorming webs enable a nonlinear thinking process that is as critical as fluency in reading and writing. In this context, Hyerle (1996) believes that "fluency is the capacity to flow flexibly from idea to idea within and across disciplines, easily make connections among ideas, sustain inquiry over time, openly pursue alternative points of view, question and possibly discard hardened opinions, and get 'unblocked' when faced with a difficult task" (p. 36).

A variety of Web sites provide examples of graphic organizers useful in Presearch, including the following:

Index of Graphic Organizers

Graphic Organizers

Graphic Organizers (NCREL)

Graphic Organizers: Write Design Online

Graphic Organizers (Kentucky Department of Education)

Inspiration® (2000) is a graphics software program that allows teachers and students to make brainstorming webs using the computer as a tool. Students can apply a graphics library and an array of shapes and colors to develop creative mind maps. The software includes a very useful collection of templates that show a collection of graphic organizers related to various disciplines (e.g., a Language Arts Character Chart, a Cause and Effect Chart for Social Studies, or a Thinking Venn Diagram). *Kidspiration*™ (2001) is similar to *Inspiration* but was specifically developed for primary students. The software has lots of graphics to combine with text to construct organizers that help students write and think.

Questioning

We have examined using general resources as part of Presearch to help students see the big picture for their topic and using tools to look at the relationships between topics, but at some point students must focus and develop research questions, or a response to the question, "What do I really want to know about my topic?" The final step in Presearch is to write a research question or focus question. Teachers and library media specialists may need to guide the development of focus questions for younger students. Good research questions should require critical thinking. Students should not move on from Presearch without developing research questions.

Writing research questions takes practice and experience, and teachers should give students ample opportunities to practice. *Questioning Toolkit,* by Jamie McKenzie, provides examples of different types of questions that teachers might use to develop lessons about questioning.

Many inquiry learning experiences require students to work in cooperative small groups. As they conceptualize their project, exploring subtopics, questioning, and focusing, they need technology tools that will enable this collaborative thinking process. Resources such as *Inspiration* will allow them to sit around a computer and contribute to the development of a web or perhaps build a mind map, but students must be in the same space physically to complete this task. Students need Web-based software that enables synergistic thinking and allows each student to make contributions from computers that have network connections. This type of technology would enable serendipitous group knowledge construction.

SEARCH

The Web has grown over the past few years at an exponential rate. Many of us can remember a time before the Web, but for young children today the Web has always been a part of their lives. These are the children who have never experienced viewing television without a remote control for changing the channels or cooking without a microwave oven. For better or worse, the Web—or whatever it morphs (evolves) into—will be an integral part of their lives. Just like Pandora, we cannot put it back into the box. Therefore, it is critical that students learn to use the Web to their best advantage. There are millions of Web sites available today, and more are being uploaded every second. Some are fantastic resources; others are a total waste of computer memory and a person's time.

Students must employ two significant strategies to be successful searchers of the Web:

♦ They must locate information efficiently.

♦ They must evaluate information appropriately.

This section focuses on a selective sampling of resources and tools that can facilitate locating and evaluating Web-based information. A preliminary step that many information seekers skip or ignore is identifying the appropriate resource or tool for the specific information need. Often, students go to the library media center, sit down in front of a computer, and open their favorite search engine. They have given no thought to whether that is the best tool for addressing their information need and no thought to any resources that might be appropriate. That should be the first step in searching. There are many print resources in the library media center, and one of those might be the best resource for this information need. Or, if the Web is the better choice, then a specific resource (e.g., *Electric Library*, the *Internet Public Library*, or *KidsClick!*) might be more appropriate than trying to search the Web at random. With that idea in mind, we discuss examples of specific Web resources.

WEB TOOLS

The notion of a Web-based tool is an important concept for students to understand. A tool is an enabler that helps you complete a task. The number and types of tools on the Web are expanding as you read this section. For example, Web tools include search engines, subject directories, tutorials, and portals. Students need practice using tools and an understanding that Web-based tools will change over time and they will always need a working knowledge of the available Web tools.

When information seekers use Web tools to find information, they should first ask, "Where do I begin?" rather than just automatically opening their favorite search engine and keying in a search phrase. First, they should develop a focus for their information need; that is, "What do I want to know about my topic?" Then they must consider the possible array of Web tools and resources that might help them locate information related to that need. Next, information seekers should consider whether their information need is for general or more in-depth information and the type of topic for which they are searching. For example, if the topic is historical, it is very likely that the library media center's book collection will provide better resources than the Web, so the catalog would be the appropriate tool to start the search. Or, if the search topic is related to current science issues, then magazines or the Web are more current resources. In this situation, information seekers should use periodical databases (magazines) or search engines (the Web), which are both tools.

We would like to clarify a misconception that many information seekers have about finding information on the Web. Many, but not all, resources on the Web are free. A growing number of publishers and producers are placing their products on the Web with access by subscription only. For example, *World Book Encyclopedia* is now available on the Web, but there is a user fee. Many information seekers go into libraries—or use their

Web sites—and access periodical databases such as *MAS* or *Middle Search* (EBSCO) and *InfoTrac* (Gale Group). Typically, these are both a search engine and full-text resources of magazines and newspapers. Because these products are easily accessed and on the Web, many information seekers assume that they are free. Libraries often make these available through their Web sites, but information seekers must input their user names and passwords, provided by their local or state library.

Subject directories such as *Yahoo* can be very helpful early in the search process when the searcher is still seeking the general level of understanding about a topic. Web search engines take a broader swipe at the millions of potential Web sites, but they differ in their databases and functions, so an information seeker should be familiar with several search engines and give consideration to which might be the most useful before starting a search.

Library media specialists and teachers who want to help students become more efficient and effective at finding information on the Web should begin by showing students the difference between directories (e.g., *Yahoo*, *Yahooligans*, *Look Smart* and search engines (e.g., *Google*, *Excite*, *Ask Jeeves*). It is not really important that students understand the difference between directories and search engines from a structural perspective. People drive cars and use computers without an intimate knowledge of what makes them function. What is important is that information seekers understand the difference between the search strategies required to successfully find information using these tools. The Pathways model includes four search strategies under Seek Relevant Information. Two of these strategies are Hierarchical and Analytical (see Chapter 1). The Hierarchical strategy applies to a subject directory, and the Analytical strategy applies to a search engine.

A Hierarchical search requires an information seeker to know how a topic is related to other topics. For example, Jason is looking for information on tropical rain forests. His research question is, "How are the rainforests of the northwestern U.S. different from those of Brazil?" He found an article in an encyclopedia, so he has developed some background knowledge. Next, he has decided to use *Yahoo*. To successfully use *Yahoo*, a subject directory, he must be able to make selections from the subject tree. His first selection is the Science category. As each list of more focused subjects appears, he makes the following selections: >Ecology, >Ecological Systems, >Forests, and then >Rainforests. With this final decision, a list of Web links appears that are all related to rainforests; a total of 71 references. This is a more manageable number of Web resources than what might result from using a search engine.

Jason may decide that he wants to narrow the search focus to the animals that are native to the rain forests of the Pacific Northwest, and at that point he does need to use a search engine. The search engine will allow him to input a specific search phrase, which must be carefully constructed, or he may get an unmanageable results list.

Many information seekers are challenged when they try to find information on the Web. They often do not have the knowledge and experience to make the decisions about appropriate resources and tools that will help them find the best information about their topic. The Web has grown at an incredible rate but is still in its infancy. Information seekers need tools that are actually advance organizers to provide them with clues to help them make the right decisions.

Subject Directories

The line between subject directories and search engines has blurred somewhat because most subject directories also include a search engine on their home page, and many search engines include a subject directory on their home page. Typically, the search engine on a directory site is not as powerful as a separate search engine. The reverse is also true: The subject directories located on search engine pages are more simplistic than those that are primarily a subject directory. *Yahoo* is the most popular subject directory, with a significant number of subjects in the various levels of the subject tree. *Yahooligans* is a subject directory for young people with subjects that appeal to a younger age level. The *Study Web* by Lightspan is a subject directory based on subjects that are typical to a K–12 school curriculum, based on a collection of more than 160,000 reviewed Web links.

Search Engines

Search engines are software that use the search query of an information seeker to look through huge databases that contain information about Web sites and select only those sites that match the query. This process generates the results list. Many search engines offer the option of using natural language or Boolean searching. If an information seeker is doing a natural language search, she would input a phrase or sentence into the search box. The software discards common words (e.g., articles, conjunctions, prepositions) and then looks through the database using the remaining words as the search query.

Google, *AltaVista*, and *Ask Jeeves* all include this feature in their search function. Often, this natural language feature does return a useable hit list, and the search engines tend to sort this list in order of revelance, so those Web links that appear at the top of the hit list may be the information needed.

This is not always the case, however. Sometimes an advanced search is required to narrow the focus, and thus the hit list, down to a more manageable number of Web resources. *AltaVista* allows the information seeker to use natural language or an advanced search with Boolean operators. The software also provides options for filtering the search results by date and language. For example, an information seeker might search *AltaVista* for information on "presidential elections prior to 2000" and in the "Spanish language," putting these two phrases in brackets. *AltaVista* would search the database using this search phrase and return a results list.

Boolean logic (AND, OR, NOT) is part of the Analytical search strategy of Pathways. Someday these search engines may include sophisticated expert systems that will negate the need for information seekers to be able to construct an analytical search, but that is not the case today. Students should not leave high school without this skill because they will need it in the working world. Learning to use Boolean logic is a matter of practice and experience. One of the best books for teaching students to use Boolean logic is *Decision Points* (Houghton and Houghton, 1999).

Students tend to have only a surface level of knowledge about the features and functions of search engines. Some search engines are very sophisticated and have the capability to provide focused information, but students do not know how to use their features. Their results lists are long and general rather than short, focused, and relevant to their information need or research question. It is not necessary for students to know how to use many search engines. They would be more efficient searchers if they knew several search engines well but also knew the strengths of those search engines, so that they would be prepared to select the right one when they have a specific information need.

The best way to help students become acquainted with several search engines is to give a searching assignment and then work with them as they select the keywords to use as part of the search query. Require students to keep a record of their results lists using a specific set of keywords and then compare the results across several search engines. Repeat this exercise enough times so students can begin to see differences in the features of each search engine and the differences in the results lists in terms of relevance to topic and quality of information. Eventually, students should begin to see patterns that show which search engines have a greater focus on specific topics and/or the unique features of the search engines. Each of the search engines has strengths and weaknesses in subject areas, depending on those Web sites contained in the databases. The *Search Engine Watch* Web site reviews and compares search engines.

Search engines are constantly evolving and changing for the better. As we write this chapter, *Google* is our search engine of choice; in six months or a year, another search engine may come along with newer and better features. *AltaVista* and *HotBot* are also well-respected search engines. Some search engines are known for their special features. For example, *Ask Jeeves* and *Ask Jeeves for Kids* use questions as the search query. The results list is returned in a question format. The *Vivisimo* meta search engine returns the results in clusters within folders that are subtopics of the original search query, which becomes an organizational strategy. *Vivisimo* also offers the option to open the Web site in a new window, a full window, or preview.

Organizing Information

There is more to searching than just finding information. The Web is vast, and the amount of information that can be retrieved from it is mind boggling. Organizing information is a formidable challenge. One search engine that helps searchers organize their information is *iLOR*, which is powered by *Google*. This search engine attempts to facilitate the organization of those Web sites that are selected from the results list. Selected Web sites can be placed in a personal list, opened but dropped to the task bar, or opened in another window. A fourth option allows the user to drop an anchor on the search results page, then open the selected link and explore the new site. When exploration is completed, the anchor, residing in a small box on the top left side of the screen, returns the user to the *iLOR* search results page. Each referenced link on *iLOR* includes three link options: (1) link to a similar site, (2) the option to view the Web page as originally searched by *iLOR*, and (3) links to other pages that have linked to the page within the results list. The link to a similar site is especially useful because this becomes a very focused search without the searcher having to provide the search phrases.

Search engine developers understand that they must continually move forward in terms of new features and functions. One of the next steps for development in search engine functionality is in the area of user friendliness.

Tutorials

Web sites that are tutorials or guides for Web searching are available to help those information seekers who find search engines to be complicated and get results lists that are not relevant and are much too long.

NoodleTools was developed by Debbie Abilock and her son, Damon. This partnership combined Debbie's experience working with students who need to find information for reports and projects with Damon's skills in designing creative Web tools. *NoodleTools* includes

NoodleBib (a wizard for creating bibliographies),

NoodleQuest (a wizard for developing a search strategy),

NoodleLinks (a database of bibliographies), and

NoodleBoard (an electronic bulletin board for sharing ideas with others).

NoodleQuest uses questions to focus the search topic of an information seeker. The responses to these questions enable the software to produce a profile of information that will help the information seeker begin his or her search. *NoodleBib* is a very useful tool because it helps students develop and maintain the citation information for the resources used in papers and projects.

A growing number of Web-based tutorials provide instruction on Web searching, including using subject directories and search engines. One of the best is *KidsClick!* Select "Search Lessons" at the top of the home page. Lesson topics include keyword searching, Boolean logic, database structure, and filtering issues. Other Web sites also provide descriptive and evaluative information about specific search engines and subject directories. Information seekers can find search tips and tutorials on planning a search strategy; these sites include

Web Searching,

Searchopolis, and

The Spider's Apprentice.

The technical terms used on Web sites can be confusing for novice information seekers. The *Glossary of Terms* on the *SeekHelp.com* Web site provides a comprehensive list of Web-related words with definitions.

Web Resources for Locating Information

Although the Web has millions of Web sites, only a fraction of those contain reliable and useable information. One difference between a Web-based resource and a print resource (books and magazines) is the way in which each is published. Books and magazines are usually published by companies with editors who provide some type of quality control over the content. In contrast, anyone with some knowledge of Web authoring software and access to a Web server can publish a Web site, bypassing the quality control system of print resources. That does not mean that print resources are all wonderful and that Web resources are all bad, but information seekers should exercise some degree of caution when gathering information from the Web.

Types of Resources

There are many different types of resources on the Web. In this section we focus on virtual libraries, portals, virtual field trips, experts, and primary source documents.

Virtual Libraries

Virtual libraries are collections of electronic resources based on specified selection criteria. These are becoming more numerous on the Web. Virtual libraries provide a way of focusing students on a selective collection and avoiding some of the less appropriate sites on the Web.

KidsClick! is a virtual library of Web resources appropriate for students and teachers; it is selected and maintained by the librarians at the Colorado State Library. The selection policy criteria are posted on the site. Conceptually, it is important to think of this Web site as a virtual library collection and another part of your library media center's collection. The site also has links to several image and clip art collections that are appropriate for young students. In addition, there is an audio section with links to sites with speeches, animal sounds, and national anthems.

School library media center collections are developed based on selection criteria. Many library media specialists today are developing virtual library collections on their Web sites that add Web resources to their collections. Some library media specialists have developed these collections based on the same selection criteria they use for their site-based collections; others have developed different selection criteria for the Web resources. This type of virtual library adds appropriate resources to the library media center collection and helps students and teachers access Web information more efficiently.

Schools, districts, and states have created virtual libraries. Following are examples:

◆ *Your Virtual IMC.* The Centerville City Schools (Ohio) Central Resource Center Director, Chris Findlay, has created a virtual library for the district that includes Web access to each of the district school catalogs, subscription resources, literature resources, and so forth.

◆ *Chico High School* (California). Peter Milbury's virtual library is an example of an extensive LMC Web resource collection.

◆ *North Junior High School Library Media Center Web* (Minnetonka, Minnesota) site is also a rich virtual library.

◆ *Sunlink* is an example of a state virtual library; it includes all the resources in Florida's elementary and secondary schools.

Portals

Lightspan, *Discovery School*, and *BigChalk* portals provide access to resources and information for the school community. These services also enable communication between students, teachers, administrators, and parents with features like the electronic bulletin boards, e-mail, and chat. The portal software is typically free and resides either on the school district's server or the portal's server. Communication is limited to those who are in the community, with user names and passwords. Portals also focus on the resource and tool needs of students, teachers, and parents, including subscription services to Web-based references. For example, *BigChalk* has a resource collection that includes *ProQuest*, *Electric Library*, *Literature Online* (LION), and *Encarta Encyclopedia Deluxe*. The *BigChalk* universal search engine, Retriever, searches all of the resources and produces a results list that reflects information in all of them. *BigChalk* also offers functions that help students organize information. Results lists provide a feature that allows students to select titles and add them to a personal list.

Experts

A unique advantage of the Web is the ability to connect students with people who are experts in their field. The Web transcends distance and position and enables conversations through e-mail and discussion forums. For example, *Journey North* engages students in tracking the migration of a variety of species, including the monarch butterfly. Students who are involved with this project have opportunities to question the scientists who maintain the project. The *eNature.com* Web site provides students with access to the scientists who are part of that project. *Ask an Expert* is a Web site that provides access to many people who are experts in their fields. Many sections of the *Yahoo* directory include an expert category.

Virtual Field Trips

The Web offers many opportunities to take virtual field trips, such as trips to museums around the world, visits to historical sites, journeys to other lands, and voyages to sites that might be considered inaccessible or inappropriate for students to visit. Some examples follow:

♦ At *British Museum* students can take a virtual tour of the Cleopatra of Egypt exhibit.

♦ *Louvre Museum* provides virtual tours of various galleries.

♦ *Exploratorium* takes students on tours of creative science discoveries, with a focus on inquiry.

♦ *Franklin Institute Online* offers virtual tours of science exhibits,

♦ *The Battle of Gettysburg, 1863: Eyewitness* allows visitors to "see" the Battle of Gettysburg through the diary entries of Tillie Pierce, a young resident of Gettysburg in 1863.

♦ *Tower of London* shows visitors English history through the eyes of a tour guide.

Searching on "virtual field trips" in *Google* or other search engines results in a significant list of Web sites. To find virtual field trips in *Yahoo*, select >Recreation, >Travel, and >Virtual Field Trips.

Primary Source Documents

Primary source documents are among the most exciting resources on the Web today. Primary source documents are original documents, often created by people who held government positions or participated in historical events. They include historical maps, diaries, journals, letters, speeches, treaties, and photographs. A journal written by a person living through a historical event can provide insight into that event that might never have been included in history textbooks. The diary entries of Tillie Pierce mentioned in the section above are an example of a primary source document. These documents allow students of today to draw their own conclusions about historical events. Examples of primary documents on the Web are the following:

◆ *Valley of the Shadow*. This is a rich collection of primary source documents from the Civil War period that reflect the perspectives of people who lived in two towns; one on the Northern side and the other on the Southern side of the war.

◆ *Presidential Libraries*. The historical documents from the past presidents of the United States in the last half of the twentieth century are available at this site, thanks to the efforts of the National Archives and Records Administration.

◆ *Perseus Digital Library* is another rich source of documents, with a special focus on the ancient world.

Information seekers looking for primary source documents can find many Web sites by searching in *Google* or other search engines under "primary source documents."

Primary source documents can be a challenge for students because the text can be technical and/or a reflection of the time period. For example, people used the English language in colonial times in America, but words sometimes had different meanings from the way we use them today, and they were often spelled differently. Handwritten documents show variations from the alphabet we consider standard today. For younger students, teachers might consider copying a sampling of the more pertinent documents (cited appropriately), pasting the text into a word processor, and increasing the type size a level or two. They could also go through each document and put a short definition in parentheses beside some of the more technical terms. Older students should be able to handle many of these documents with some assistance from teachers. For example, teachers could ask students to underline those words that are unfamiliar, then hold a discussion on how our language has changed over time.

Evaluating Information

Evaluating Web-based information is a critical part of the research process. Previously in the Search section we mentioned the issue of quality in regard to information available on the Web. Students who are gathering information for papers and projects must have a healthy level of skepticism about information they find on the Web. Unfortunately, many people, students included, are enamored by the glamour and glitz of the Web and seem to feel that any information they find must be accurate and useful. Wrong!

First, it is important to consider the source of the information. Web sites are produced by individuals, educational institutions (.edu), government agencies (.gov), associations (.org), and commercial entities (.com). The suffixes listed here appear after the name of the Internet Service Provider (ISP) on a Web address. For example, Web sites that are stored on servers at the University of Northern Iowa would have the following address: http://www.uni.edu. The "uni" tells us that the server is located at the University of Northern Iowa, and the "edu" indicates that the ISP is an educational institution. The same pattern works for the other suffixes.

The internal and external links on a Web site can inform us about the accuracy and integrity of the information on the site. Web sites with a majority of links that are internal should show a red flag because that suggests that the ideas on that site are primarily those of the Web author. This is similar to an article or book that has no references to other writers who can substantiate that information. It is important to pay attention to the external links on a Web site because sometimes these support biased or inaccurate information on the home site.

A good rule to follow is to always substantiate the information found in one resource with that found in another resource. AND, find that other resource independent of the first resource. In other words, do not use an external link from one resource to find another resource if your goal is to substantiate information. Accuracy, bias, and perspective are all issues when gathering information from a Web site. Finding the same information on another Web site is a useful strategy to check accuracy.

Bias and perspective are not the same. The *Encarta World English Dictionary* (2001) defines *bias* as "an unfair preference for or dislike of something" and *perspective* as an "evaluation of a situation or facts, especially from that person's point of view." A person might be biased for or against a political party but might have a different perspective on a party's position on taxation.

Relevance is another important criterion for evaluating information. For example, a student was searching an electronic encyclopedia for information on animals, such as cats, dogs, and horses. When the software returned a results list, the first one at the top of the list was about the musical group, "The Animals." In this situation, the student printed the information and then left for his classroom without ever considering whether the information was related to his research topic. Unfortunately, this is a very typical scenario. Relevance requires checking the information to be sure it relates to the research topic or question.

Some Web sites offer checklists, rubrics, and activities for teachers and students to focus on evaluating Web-based information. It is important to remember that evaluating information is not limited to Web resources.

Joyce Valenza created *A WebQuest About Evaluating Web Sites* for high school students. This would be a valuable learning experience for students because they engage in comparing the information from Web sites all focused on the same topics. The student materials include a Web evaluation form and a rubric for assessing students.

Checklists are good tools for helping students evaluate their Web-based sources of information. A checklist that has been developed using fun cartoon characters and a quiz format is *The Quality Information Checklist*. It was developed for middle school students and has seven questions with multiple-choice answers. The site is animated and interactive. There is an excellent teacher's guide on this Web site with background information on evaluating the information on Web sites and a list of links to other Web sites that provide similar information. Other examples of evaluation checklists can be found on *Kathy Schrock's Guide for Educators*.

Sometimes it's a challenge to convince students that information that is totally inaccurate and/or biased exists on the Web. Kathy Schrock has provided an excellent list of Web sites that showcase this type of information at the very bottom of the Critical Evaluation Information page. Such Web sites are valuable teaching tools.

Final Thoughts on Searching Tools

Finding relevant and appropriate information on the Web is a challenge for all information seekers, but an even greater challenge is organizing the mountain of information obtained to make sense of it. Organization includes note taking, but this is not just copying the information, regardless of whether students obtain a printer copy or record information in their own words. Students need templates or organizers that guide their note taking with reflective questions and a structure that can be diminished as students learn the skill of note taking. These should not be considered worksheets on which students simply parrot back answers to questions, but rather guides to helping students think critically about the information they have located. Students need these note taking guides in an electronic format that is dynamic, allows for multiple student input, and is stored on the Web for access from home, library, or classroom.

As the information explosion continues, driven by the ever-changing environment of technology and expert systems, students will find themselves drowning in an information ocean. They will need the tools to establish information need profiles so that only the most useful and relevant information arrives in their work and/or home workstations. Push technology, a service that provides personalized information, is still in its infancy. Web-based companies like *Yahoo* are now offering personal portals that include information that arrives on a Web page based on the profile information provided by that individual. Developing that information profile so the portal can provide the relevant and appropriate information is another skill students must learn in the future.

INTERPRETATION

Interpretation is the scaffold between gathering the information and using it in a meaningful way. Often, students gather information for a research paper or project and move immediately to writing the paper or constructing the project. They still have raw information because they have not taken the time to develop their own understanding of that information.

There are many tools students can use to assess the usefulness of their information and develop personal meaning. Most of these tools are graphic organizers that allow students to visualize relationships between information or see patterns that emerge from information. One of the most important tools for interpreting information is *Inspiration*, which we have mentioned in many other places in this book. *Inspiration* is unique software and has many different applications within the information search process. In the Interpretation stage of Pathways, the template library within the software is very valuable. For example, there is a template of a comparison chart that allows comparison of events, people, or issues. Other organizers in the template library are cause and effect; history webs; an idea map; and a Venn diagram.

The Venn diagram is an organizer that has application across all the Pathways stages. However, Venn diagrams really shine in the Interpretation stage because they show "relationships, draw conclusions, make inferences or organize the material to help communicate" (Jay, 2000).

There are many examples of graphic organizers on the Web; some were covered in the Presearch section. However, it seems appropriate here to refocus on some of those same Web sites to highlight the organizers that would be especially useful in Interpretation. *The Index of Graphic Organizers* includes examples of organizers that can be used for classifying, sequencing, showing cause and effect, and comparisons. The *Graphic Organizers* Web site by Write Design Online includes examples of organizers for sequencing, fishbone map, and spider map (analysis). *Printables: Graphic Organizers* has many examples of organizers that would enable students to interpret their information. These organizers open in *Adobe Acrobat Reader* and can be printed.

An important part of constructing new knowledge is reflection. An instructional strategy to foster reflective writing is journaling. Journals can be a challenge to assess. There are no Web tools available at this writing that would enable a formal journaling process. Teachers need software that is Web-based so it can be accessed from students' homes, the library media center, or the classroom. This software might be part of a student's portal and accessible by the teacher for periodic reading.

One Web-based tool that is used for many online teaching situations is the discussion forum. *WebCT* and *Blackboard* have an electronic discussion by topic feature that allows for a threaded discussion and can be kept private by using user names and passwords. Teachers who instruct online use guided questions to foster discussions, and often the responses by students are thoughtful and reflective. Such software can be used for learning experiences beyond formal courses. For example, library media specialists might consider using this software for online book clubs. Students could use the discussion forums to have conversations about the books they read.

COMMUNICATION

The Communication stage allows students to apply new information to solve a problem or share their new knowledge with others. The Web offers opportunities for students to develop and exhibit their work, develop Web-based slide shows on various topics, design information quests, use tutorials for application programs, and design their own Web sites. The following list provides some examples of these communication tools:

♦ Original Exhibits

   Cyberkids publishes original works submitted by young people aged seven to twelve on their Web site.

   Kids' Space provides students with opportunities to exhibit their creative works. Students can exhibit stories, music, pictures, poetry, multimedia projects, and so forth on two Web sites.

♦ Slide Shows

   Trackstar allows teachers and students to create annotated slide shows of Web sites based on a specific topic. Web sites are selected and placed in the software with a navigational bar that enables users to move back and forth. The bar also includes space for descriptive text and/or questions about the Web site. The sites are still active so that users can open all the links but remain within the slide show function.

♦ Quests

WebQuests engage students in creative and engaging tasks with a focus on gathering information rather than on finding resources. Either teachers or students can design WebQuests. Typically, the resources are Web-based, although that is not a requirement, and they have already been identified before students begin the project. Students could easily design WebQuests as a concluding project in a unit. Several Web sites are available to help teachers and students as they design WebQuests, including *The WebQuest Page*, and the *Knowledge Network Explorer*. Each of these sites reflects the presence of Bernie Dodge, who, along with Tom March, conceived the idea of WebQuests a few years ago. These Web sites have information about WebQuests, tips for developing a WebQuest, and templates to help you get started.

ThinkQuests offer lots of possibilities for sharing new knowledge. A ThinkQuest is a Web-based project that engages students in an in-depth study of a topic. Typically, students work in small groups on a ThinkQuest. The *ThinkQuest* Web site has many resources, tips, and tutorials for developing a ThinkQuest. There are annual contests for ThinkQuests, and the winners are posted on this site. The *ThinkQuest* Web site has been set up as a community, so members who are registered have access to a threaded bulletin board, private e-mail, and a chat room.

♦ Application Tutorials

Adventures of CyberBee has a section of "How Tos" that includes various tutorials about popular application software, including *Microsoft Word*, *Dreamweaver*, *Netscape*, *PowerPoint*, and *Web Construction*.

♦ Web Design

The Teachers.Net Homepage Maker is a template with many options for creating a Web page.

School Home Page Building Blocks discusses the purpose, content, design, organization, and resources for developing a Web site.

Web Monkey for Kids has lots of instructions for students and parents to help them develop simple Web pages.

The tools in this section represent the types of tools available today. Students need tools that will allow them to create projects and products collaboratively with other students who may or may not be classmates in the same school. Collaboration with students across different parts of our country or in other countries poses some exciting learning possibilities, but students in this type of learning experience can never meet face-to-face, so they need the ability to work on the same project via a Web site. They must be able to communicate with each other using tools like chats and threaded discussions. Ultimately, they need the ability to communicate in media that allow them to see and talk with each other as they are jointly working on their project. The technology for this type of communication is available now, but it requires very sophisticated technology and Internet connections that schools often do not have available. Therefore, educators should encourage those who produce software to focus on this type of tool, along with more reliable and faster Internet access.

EVALUATION

The Evaluation stage of the Pathways model focuses on students in the form of peer- and self-assessment of the process they followed in gathering and using information. This stage also focuses on evaluation of the product. This evaluation process should have been occurring throughout the other stages of Pathways. Graphic organizers, logs, journals, reflective writing, and portfolios are all strategies that enable students to evaluate their own process and teachers to assess the process.

Rubrics and checklists are good instruments for assessing product and process (see Figure B.2 in Appendix B). The *RubiStar* Web site has wizards for templates and checklists that would be helpful for teachers who want to use these tools for evaluation.

There is minimal Web-based software available to enable the self-evaluation of process by students and assessment by teachers. This is an area that really needs attention by software producers. Students need the ability to record reflection as they work and easily store it in a serendipitous manner. Teachers must be able to access these reflections and easily provide rich feedback.

There are features that software developers could include in databases, catalogs, and other information resources or tools that would allow students and teachers to reflect on the process they used. For example, a history feature in software that tracks a search and then stores that information for a short time would enable students and the teacher to review the search process and talk about what worked and what did not. Students need this type of interaction and feedback so they can learn from their mistakes.

Where and when do students learn to use the tools that enable the strategies and stages of an information process like Pathways to Knowledge? Where are these skills covered within the curriculum? We hope this chapter has raised your awareness that tools will be an ever-increasing part of the lives of our students today, now, and in the future. What is your role in teaching them to know what tools to use and when tools are appropriate for gathering, evaluating, and using information?

REFERENCES

Note: All Web addresses accessed December 21, 2001.

AASL and AECT. (1998). *Information literacy standards for student learning.* Chicago: American Library Association.

Encarta World English Dictionary 2001. (2001). Microsoft Corporation. [Online]. Available: http://dictionary.msn.com/.

Houghton, J. M., and R. S. Houghton. (1999). *Decision points: Boolean logic for computer users and beginning online searchers.* Englewood, CO: Libraries Unlimited.

Hyerle, D. (1996). *Visual tools for constructing knowledge.* Alexandria, VA: Association for Supervision and Curriculum Development.

Hyerle, D. (2000). *A Field guide to using visual tools.* Alexandria, VA: Association for Supervision and Curriculum Development.

Inspiration®. (2000). Portland, OR: Inspiration Software, Inc. Available: http://www.inspiration.com

Kidspiration™. (2001). Portland, OR: Inspiration, Inc. Available: http://www.inspiration.com/productinfo/kidspiration/index.cfm

WEB RESOURCES

Note: All Web addresses accessed December 21, 2001.

Adventures of CyberBee. (2001). Linda C. Joseph. [Online]. Available: http://www.cyberbee.com/

AltaVista. (2001). AltaVista. [Online]. Available: http://www.altavista.com/

Ask an Expert. Stevens Institute of Technology. (1998–2001). [Online]. Available: http://njnie.dl.stevens-tech.edu/askanexpert.html

Ask Jeeves. (1996–2001). Ask Jeeves. [Online]. Available: http://www.ask.com/

Ask Jeeves for Kids. (1996–2001). Ask Jeeves. [Online]. Available: http://www.ajkids.com/

The Author Corner. (n.d.). Mona Kerby. Westminster, MD: Carroll County Public Library. [Online]. Available: http://www.carr.org/authco/index.htm

Awesome Library. (1996–2001). EDI & R. Jerry Adams. [Online]. Available: http://www.awesomelibrary.org/

The Battle of Gettysburg, 1863: Eyewitness. (1997). Ibis Communications. [Online]. Available: http://www.ibiscom.com/gtburg.htm

BigChalk™. (2001). [Online]. Available: http://schools.bigchalk.com/portal

Blackboard. (2001). Blackboard. [Online]. Available: http://www.blackboard.com/

British Museum. (n.d.). [Online]. Available: http://www.thebritishmuseum.ac.uk/

The Children's Museum of Indianapolis. (2000). [Online]. Available: http://www.childrensmuseum.org/index2.htm

Coretta Scott King Award. (2000). American Library Association. [Online]. Available: http://www.ala.org/srrt/csking/cskawin.html

Cyberkids. (1999–2001). Able Minds. [Online]. Available: http://www.cyberkids.com /we/

Discovery School. (2000). Discovery. [Online]. Available: http://school.discovery.com/

Dragonfly. (2001). Christopher R. Wolfe. Oxford, OH: Miami University. [Online]. Available: http://miavx1.acs.muohio.edu/~Dragonfly/

Electric Library. (2001). Infonautics. [Online]. Available: http://ask.elibrary.com/

eNature.com. (2000). eNature. [Online]. Available: http://www.enature.com/.

Encarta. (2001). Microsoft Corporation. [Online]. Available: http://encarta.msn.com/

Excite. (2001). The Excite Network. [Online]. Available: http://my.excite.com/myexcite /my.jsp

Exploratorium. (n.d.). The Exploratorium. [Online]. Available: http://www.exploratorium .edu/

Filamentality. (1996–2001). Pacific Bell. [Online]. Available: http://www.kn.pacbell .com/wired/fil/

Franklin Institute Online. (1995–2001). The Franklin Institute Online. [Online]. Available: http://sln.fi.edu/

Glossary of terms. (1997). American Systems and DP Directory. [Online]. Available: http://www.seekhelp.com/glossary.htm

Google. (2001). [Online]. Available: http://www.google.com/

Graphic Organizers. (n.d.). California Technology Assistance Project and California County Superintendents Educational Services Association. [Online]. Available: http://www.sdcoe.k12.ca.us/score/actbank/torganiz.htm

Graphic Organizers. (n.d.). Kentucky Department of Education. [Online]. Available: http://www.kde.state.ky.us/oapd/curric/Publications/Transformations/grahicorgan .html

Graphic Organizers. (n.d.) NCREL. [Online]. Available: http://www.ncrel.org/sdrs/areas /issues/students/learning/lr1grorg.htm

Graphic Organizers. (n.d.). Write Design Online. Douglas Kipperman and Melissa McKinsley. [Online]. Available: http://www.teachervision.com/lesson-plans /lesson-6293.html

Graphic Organizers. (2000–2001). The Learning Network. [Online]. Available: http://www.teachervision.com/lesson-plans/lesson-6293.html

Helpful Bookmarks @ the C.H.S. Library. (n.d.) Peter Milbury. [Online]. Available: http://dewey.chs.chico.k12.ca.us/

HotBot. (2001). Lycos, Inc. [Online]. Available: http://hotbot.lycos.com

Index of graphic organizers. (n.d.) Greg Freeman. [Online]. Available. Http://www.graphic
.org/goindex.html

Internet Public Library. (n.d.). University of Michigan School of Information and Bell &
Howell Information and Learning. [Online]. Available: http://www.ipl.org/

Journey North: A Global Study of Wildlife Migration. (2000). Annenberg/CPB. [On-
line]. Available: http://www.learner.org/jnorth/

Kathy Schrock's Guide for Educators: Critical Evaluation Information. (2001). Discov-
ery.com. [Online]. Available: http://school.discovery.com/schrockguide/eval.html

KidsClick! Web search for kids by librarians. (2001). Colorado State Library. [Online].
Available: http://sunsite.berkeley.edu/KidsClick!/

KidsClick! Worlds of Searching. (2001). Colorado State Library. [Online]. Available:
http://www.worldsofsearching.org/

Kids' Space. (1995–2001). Kids Space Foundation. [Online]. Available: http://www.kids-space
.org/index.html

Knowledge Network Explorer. (1995–2001). Pacific Bell. [Online]. Available:
http://www.filamentality.com/

Library of Congress. (n.d.). Library of Congress. [Online]. Available: http://www.loc.gov/

Lightspan. (2000). Lightspan. [Online]. Available: http://www.lightspan.com/

LookSmart. (2001). LookSmart, Ltd. [Online]. Available: http://www.looksmart.com/

Louvre Museum. (n.d.). [Online]. Available: http://www.louvre.fr/louvrea.htm

National Gallery of Art. (2001). National Gallery of Art. [Online]. Available:
http://www.nga.gov/

Navigator. (2000). New York Times. [Online]. Available: http://www.nytimes.com
/learning/general/navigator/index.html

NoodleBib. See *NoodleTools.*

NoodleQuest. See *NoodleTools.*

NoodleTools. (1999–2001). Debbie and Damon Abilock. [Online]. Available:
http://www.noodletools.com/
(Tools include NoodleBib and NoodleQuest.)

North Junior High School Library Media Center. (n.d.). Minnetonka, MN. [Online].
Available: http://www.hopkins.k12.mn.us/pages/north/mediacenter/index.html

The Official Eric Carle Web. (n.d.). [Online]. Available: http://www.eric-carle.com/

The 100 Favorite Children's Books. (1998). The New York Public Library. [Online]. Available: http://www.nypl.org/branch/kids/100/animal.html

"On-Lion" for Kids. (November/December, 1993). New York Public Library. [Online]. Available: http://www2.nypl.org/home/branch/kids/

Presidential Libraries. (n.d.). National Archives and Records Administration (NARA). [Online]. Available: http://www.nara.gov/nara/president/address.html

Printables: Graphic Organizers. (2001). The Learning Network. [Online]. Available: http://www.teachervision.com/tv/curriculum/printables/graphics.html

ProQuest. (2001). UMI. [Online]. Available: http://www.umi.com/

The Quality Information Checklist. (2000). Showme Multimedia. [Online]. Available: http://www.quick.org.uk/menu.htm

Questioning Toolkit. (1993). Jamie McKenzie. [Online]. Available: http://questioning.org/Q7/toolkit.html

The Reading Corner. (2001). Mona Kerby. [Online]. Available: http://www.carr.org/read/index.htm

RubiStar. (2001). HPR*TEC. [Online]. Available: http://rubistar.4teachers.org/

School Home Page Building Blocks. (1998). Erica Peto and Ann McGlone. Kent School District. [Online]. Available: http://www.learningspace.org/content/default.html

Search Engine Watch. (n.d.) Internet.com. [Online]. Available: http://www.searchenginewatch.com/

Searchopolis. (1998-2000). [Online]. Available: http://www.searchopolis.com/

SeekHelp.com. (1997). American Systems. [Online]. Available: http://www.seekhelp.com

Site Evaluation Form. (1997–2001). Oregon Public Education Network. [Online]. Available: http://www.open.k12.or.us/jitt/evalform.html#UserFriendly

The Spider's Apprentice. (2001). Monash Information Services. [Online]. Available: http://www.monash.com/spidap.htm

Study Web. (1996–2000). Lightspan. [Online]. Available: http://www.studyweb.com/

Sunlink. (2000). A Project of the Florida Department of Education. [Online]. Available: http://www.sunlink.ucf.edu/default2.html

The Teachers.Net Homepage Maker. (1996–2001). Teachers.Net Web Services. [Online]. Available: http://www.teachers.net/sampler/

ThinkQuest. (1995–2001). ThinkQuest. [Online]. Available: http://www.thinkquest.org/mytq.html

Tower of London. (n.d.). [Online]. Available: http://www.tower-of-london.com/

Trackstar. (2001). HPR*TEC. [Online]. Available: http://trackstar.hprtec.org/

Virginia Hamilton's Web. (2001). Hamilton Arts. [Online]. Available: http://www.virginiahamilton.com/

Virtual Library Museum Pages. (n.d.). Jonathan Bowen. [Online]. Available: http://www.icom.org/vlmp/

The Virtual Museum for Children. (1994–1999). The Bowen Family. [Online]. Available: http://www.museums.reading.ac.uk/children/

Vivisimo. (2001). [Online]. Available: http://vivisimo.com/

Web Monkey for Kids. (2001). Wired Digital. [Online]. Available: http://hotwired.lycos.com/webmonkey/

Web Searching. (2001). Internet Public Library. [Online]. Available: http://www.ipl.org/ref/websearching.html

WebCT. (2001). WebCT. [Online]. Available: http://www.webct.com/

A WebQuest About Evaluating Web Sites. (March 2001). Joyce Valenza. [Online]. Available: http://mciunix.mciu.k12.pa.us/~spjvweb/evalwebstu.html

The WebQuest Page. (2000). San Diego State University. [Online]. Available: http://edweb.sdsu.edu/webquest/webquest.html

Yahoo! (2001). [Online]. Available: http://www.yahoo.com/

Yahooligans! (2001). Yahoo. [Online]. Available: http://www.yahooligans.com/

Young Adult Literature. (2001). Kay E. Vandergrift. [Online]. Available: http://www.scils.rutgers.edu/~kvander/YoungAdult/index.html

Your Virtual IMC. (n.d.). Chris Findlay. [Online]. Available: http://lib.centerville.k12.oh.us/

Change

Planning for Change

SETTING THE SCENE: District curriculum director decides to mandate use of an information process model.

Martha Henderson, Curriculum Director for the Thomas Chambers School District, had recently discovered the Pathways to Knowledge process model when she attended a meeting at the Department of Instruction. Two other curriculum directors were talking about their district adoptions of the Pathways model and the impact that decision had on teaching process and critical thinking. Dr. Henderson returned home and immediately requested copies of the model. She decided that the best place to introduce the Pathways model was with the social studies teachers in the middle schools. She selected one middle school, Oakville Middle School, and scheduled a meeting with the teachers.

"The eighth grade curriculum includes a research project for students. This model would really help them with their research," Dr. Henderson explained. "I would like you to use the model when you teach that unit." Dr. Henderson distributed a copy of the model to each teacher and waited while they studied it. She tried to explain the stages and strategies of the model.

"Our students already know how to use the library," said one of the teachers, Tom Mitchell. "This seems like an addition to our curriculum and it is really the responsibility of the library media specialist."

Dr. Henderson pulled out a packet from her folder. "I think this is the packet of instructions students receive when they start the research unit. It provides information on note taking, outlining, and developing a storyboard for their PowerPoint presentations, along with a Pathfinder developed by the LMS. All of this is very useful information, but it does not help students learn that gathering and using information is a process. Part of our district's new social studies curriculum focuses on process, inquiry learning, and critical thinking. That is your teaching responsibility, and this model has the potential to help you teach those concepts."

Later that same day . . .

Dr. Henderson entered the library media center just as students were departing for the day. "Hello," said Craig Williams, the LMS. "It's nice to see you in the building. What can I do for you?"

Dr. Henderson showed Craig the Pathways model and described her meeting with the social studies teachers. "Have you used this model before?" she asked.

"No, but I have heard about it. I think it is being used in a middle school near us," said Craig.

"I am excited about this model because this is a process that can be applied in all of our curricular areas. As we have been rewriting the district's curricula there is much emphasis on inquiry and critical thinking. This process model would help us implement that part of the curriculum."

"What was the reaction of the social studies teachers?" asked Craig.

"Well, to be honest, they were not very enthusiastic," said Dr. Henderson.

"I know that this is a model that is used in many schools," said Craig. "I've been thinking that we needed to put an information process model in place, so the timing might be good. We might get a more positive reception from teachers if we get them involved in a pilot project that uses this model. I know the LMS at Silver Creek Middle School in Madison County, and they are using the Pathways model. I would be willing to visit her and gather some information about how they got started using the model. We might want to arrange a field trip for some of our social studies teachers to visit their school."

"That sounds like a good plan," said Dr. Henderson. "I will wait to hear from you."

Several days later Craig was visiting with Sheila Rosemond, the LMS at Silver Creek Middle School. "These seventh-grade students are at the novice level in using the Pathways model," said Sheila. "They have had two other experiences using the model, but they still have much to learn. However, they do have a sense that this is a holistic process. They use journals as they do their projects. I give them writing prompts related to the stages and strategies they are using from the model. We always write about and discuss the process and how it worked for them. We talk about the strategies that worked and those that did not. I have worked with the English and social studies teachers, and they now integrate the model into their units whenever some form of research is required by students."

Craig decided it would be useful to bring several social studies teachers over to Silver Creek Middle School for a visit. He arranged for them to leave school early one afternoon so they could observe students using the Pathways model for research. After school they met with the Silver Creek social studies and English teachers, as well as the LMS. The Oakville teachers had many questions.

"How did you get started?"

"Did you teach specific skills as separate lessons first?"

"Who was responsible for teaching the model?"

"How do you keep track of the strategies the students know?"

"How do you assess students' ability to apply the process?"

The next week the Oakville social studies teachers met with Craig and Dr. Henderson. After some discussion they agreed to use the model in their research unit as a pilot. They spent some time discussing the criteria they would use to assess the outcome of the pilot. Then they began the planning process for their unit.

(Scenario 5.1 continues on page 102.)

Library media specialists, teachers, and administrators have approached us with the question, "How do we move from one or two people who are using inquiry learning with Pathways to a more school- or district-wide approach? Should we mandate that all teachers use the same model in one school? Use the same model across the district? How do we help teachers and library media specialists understand that inquiry learning requires a fundamental change in both the curriculum and the instructional practice?" There are several issues inherent in these questions.

First, and probably most important, is that change takes time. We mentioned Sharon Coatney, the library media specialist at Oak Hill Elementary School, in Overland Park, Kansas (see Chapter 3, Collaboration). From conversations with Sharon, we know that the exciting inquiry learning environment that is now in place in Oak Hill did not happen overnight. In fact, it took the administrators, teachers, and library media specialist approximately 10 to 12 years to achieve this level of change. The important and key element that drove that change was a consistent and sustained effort to move forward with common yet flexible goals. Coatney said there was very little turnover during that time, with the same LMS and teaching staff working on implementation. The district leadership pursued a common philosophy, and new principals were hired who had the same perspective on inquiry learning. Too often, educators have leaped into a new program, tried it for several years, then abandoned the program. If change is to work, it must be sustained over time.

In Scenario 5.1 the curriculum director, Dr. Henderson, knows that inquiry learning, process, and critical thinking are part of the district's new curriculum goals. She has discovered the Pathways model and selected a group of middle school social studies teachers to initiate the use of the model. She is pursuing change across the school district.

Sheila Rosemond, who is in another school district, is working on change within one school. Regardless of whether the change is occurring in a school or across the district, making the shift to process and inquiry is a curriculum change. Process and inquiry are only a part of a broader, more contemporary curriculum perspective that is grounded in constructivist learning theory. No matter how great the idea for change might be (e.g., a new program, different schedule, major curriculum initiative), implementation requires a well-developed plan, a supportive group to foster enthusiasm and become the advocates, buy-in from those who must implement the change, administrative support, professional development, and sustained financial support.

CURRICULUM CHANGE FROM THE TRADITIONAL TO THE CONTEMPORARY

Figure 5.1 shows seven target indicators for curriculum change, with criteria that reflect traditional teacher-centered curriculum, contemporary teacher/student-centered curriculum, and contemporary student-centered curriculum. The seven target indicators, when considered as a holistic change, represent significant new knowledge and skills for both teachers and students. It is also important to consider that teachers may already be practicing some parts of this contemporary approach to curriculum design, at least in the middle column, teacher/student centered. When educators talk about changing the curriculum, they often do not recognize that all these indicators are affected within that change process.

It is also important to understand that contemporary curriculum design is based on constructivist learning theory, which is discussed briefly in Chapter 2 (see Figure 2.1). This Learning Theory chart shows some of the differences between traditional (behaviorism) and contemporary (constructivism) curriculum design. The Contemporary Curriculum Design diagram (see Figure 2.2) shows constructivist learning theory as the umbrella, with the various contemporary curriculum designs (e.g., authentic learning, problem-based learning) as the spokes of the umbrella. Learning styles, multiple intelligences, brain-based, and inquiry are the supports for those curriculum designs. With this background in mind, we focus briefly on the indicators in the rubric shown in Figure 5.1.

Critical Thinking

The traditional model for curriculum design was developed for learners who often work in factories. This is the assembly line approach to learning. All the widgets are the same and must go through the same hole. Many students (not all of course) became workers who held jobs in a work environment where they were expected to follow orders and minimal thinking was required of them. The working world that our students move into after graduation today is very different. Business and industrial leaders tell us they need workers who are critical thinkers and creative; who can think about, and solve, problems that are related to customers and products. The development of critical thinking requires practice and experience. Learning activities that are focused on rote memory or spewing back facts in response to test questions do not provide practice for critical thinking. Learners need opportunities to apply knowledge to a problem or evaluate various options and then reach a conclusion or decision.

Figure 5.1. Curriculum Change: Traditional to Contemporary.

Curriculum Change:
Traditional to Contemporary

Traditional → Contemporary

Target Indicators	Teacher Centered	Teacher/Student Centered	Student Centered
Critical Thinking	Fact based, knowledge level, recall of facts.	Explaining; some analysis and evaluation. →	Analysis, evaluation, and synthesis. Students can interpret, apply, see various perspectives, transformation of thinking.
Depth of Content Knowledge	Expectations of content knowledge tend to be broad but shallow. Assignments are look-up tasks.	Focus is on disparate activities that are theme based; lacks focus on big ideas. Units often reflect look-up tasks. →	Learners are engaged in learning the big ideas through essential questions.
Assessment	Student knowledge evaluated through objective tests. No assessment of process.	Student knowledge evaluated; objective tests and projects. →	Assessment of content through demonstration of new knowledge.
Authentic Context	Learning is classroom and school bound.	Learning uses multiple resources, experts, learning community. →	Learning reflects a broad connection to the world we live in.
Learner Choice and Engagement	Learners seldom have meaningful choices.	Learner choice frequently occurs but topics, ideas, themes are teacher driven. Products are typically assigned. →	Learners have meaningful choices. Learners engage in problem/questions/ issues, topic development and make decisions about strategies for resolution.
Interactive Knowledge Construction	Learning is focused on the individual, with little interaction between learners.	Learners work cooperatively in groups to develop projects or activities. →	Interaction within student groups with a common task or problem that requires the synergy of group members to complete.
Inquiry as Process	Steps for gathering and using information are typically focused on specific resources and teacher driven. Little evidence of basic level of information literacy standards.	Use of multiple resources is encouraged. Some evidence of process application apparent. Evidence of novice and some proficient level with information literacy standards. →	Students independently apply a process approach and demonstrate a proficient or exemplary level for the information literacy standards.

Depth of Content Knowledge

The traditional approach to curriculum design was (is) textbook based, and assignments were and perhaps still are look-up activities. One of the classic examples of a look-up assignment is the States Unit. Students go to the library with a worksheet and look up the state flower, the state flag, the state bird, and so forth. This is a knowledge level assignment, with no evidence of critical thinking. The traditional curriculum also tends to be shallow but broad in scope.

Although the national standards have changed in recent years, previous approaches to the social studies curriculum were exemplified in the way U.S. history was covered. The curriculum started with the day Christopher Columbus arrived on North American shores (questionable) and theoretically covered our country's historical development into modern times. We use the word "theoretically" because, in practice, most history courses devoted a great deal of time to the American Revolution and the Civil War, and the twentieth century was often covered in haste. Today, in an effort to allow for greater depth in a more focused approach to social studies, U.S. history is spread out over several years of study, with little or no recursive time spent on previous time periods.

Curriculum and standards today tend to be based on goals and benchmarks that focus more on concepts rather than on specific facts. Contemporary curriculum is often designed using concepts or essential questions rather than measurable objectives. Content is much more focused and often crosses disciplines.

At the elementary level there is more of a focus on thematic units today, which reflects elements of contemporary curriculum design. Students tend to like units that have a theme and engage them in a variety of activities. The Colonial Fair Unit is a good example. Students learn to make products typical of colonial times (e.g., soap, candles), learn songs and dances typical of the time period, experience a day in the life of a colonial child attending school, and so forth. Although all these activities are fun and interesting and have the advantage of fostering student mental engagement, the question is, what big ideas do they learn? What is the depth of content knowledge here?

Assessment

There is a difference between assessment and evaluation, although many educators use the two words interchangeably. Jean Donham has been an active voice for assessment over evaluation, especially where this affects process. She explains the difference between evaluation and assessment as follows:

> Evaluation has traditionally occurred at the end of a learning episode. Its primary intent has been to place a value on the student's work ex post facto. Often, its ultimate purpose is to sort students according to their degree of success. Assessment represents a shift toward using a process to guide learning. As a participant in the process, students can develop skill in assessing their own progress—an important aspect of becoming self-regulated, life-long learners. (Donham, 1998, p. 6)

In the traditional curriculum the assumption is that there is a confined body of knowledge, students can learn this body of knowledge (memorize), and teachers can test this knowledge using objective tests.

Assessment in the contemporary curriculum may sometimes include a test, but the notion of a confined body of knowledge becomes cloudy when students are learning based on concepts or big ideas. Individual or student groups may focus on related areas but not necessarily cover the same content. Because all students do not cover exactly the same content, an objective test is problematic. Beyond that issue, assessment is focused on students' ability to demonstrate their new knowledge in relation to the essential questions. Typically, this involves some type of product or task. In this type of curriculum, design assessment is ongoing and uses more than one form of measurement. Reflection and journaling are often used because these forms of writing help students construct new understandings. Portfolios of student work allow students and the teacher to see progress over time.

Assessment includes both content and process. Because the curriculum includes a focus on information literacy and a process model, there must be a strategy for assessing process. As students gradually become more experienced with applying the stages of the Pathways model to their research projects, both teacher assessment of this process and student self-evaluation should take place.

Authentic Context

The traditional curriculum was typically delivered in a closed school environment. The school was where learning occurred. Today, with the arrival of technology and connections to the Internet, learning can occur anywhere. This has brought about a change in curriculum design to include many more connections to the world outside of school. However, technology alone did not foster this change to an authentic perspective in curriculum design. Among cognitive psychologists who developed constructivism, from the writings of John Dewey and Jean Piaget to current voices such as Ted Sizer and Howard Gardner, the emphasis has been on a more experiential approach to learning. They have encouraged educators to make learning more relevant and practical for students, which means connections to the world outside the school building.

The learning environment for an authentic context is the learning community and beyond. The Internet opens the door to global communication and learning experiences. Within the school itself students need access to multiple resources, with less emphasis placed on textbooks in each subject for every child. Contemporary curriculum design requires a library media center that is the learning laboratory for the curriculum. In the traditional approach, library resources were a nice extra but not essential for the learning program. Textbooks and teacher lectures filled that need. That is not the case in the contemporary model. Access to information in all types of formats becomes an imperative for students and teachers.

Learner Choice and Engagement

The issue of getting students' attention so that they are focused on a learning experience is not new with contemporary curriculum design. That is a problem that educators have known probably forever. Contemporary curriculum design, and specifically inquiry learning, place special emphasis on learner engagement: the act of motivating students so they become mentally engaged in a learning activity and thus have buy-in with the concepts or essential questions.

The traditional model puts the teacher in control of the learning experience for students. The traditional teacher is the deliverer of content, along with the textbook. Students receive explicit instructions on assignments and papers and are not in a decision-making position in terms of their own learning experiences. This is a passive approach to learning. In the contemporary model, active learning is encouraged. In this model, students have responsibility for their own knowledge construction; the teacher is not responsible for pouring knowledge into them. The teacher becomes a facilitator and coach as students gather information from multiple resources, organize that information in ways that allow them to construct new understandings, and demonstrate their new knowledge in relation to the original essential questions developed by the teacher.

This becomes student-centered learning, which does not mean that the teacher has no role in defining the learning experiences for students. There is clearly a district and/or state curriculum that must be followed, so the teacher designs a unit that reflects those goals or standards but structures the learning experiences so students have meaningful choices. Obviously, there will be differences between the type of choices that first-grade students might have and those established for high school students. Student choice means slowly giving students responsibility for their own learning over time and holding them accountable for those choices in relation to their own knowledge construction.

Interactive Knowledge Construction

Interactivity among students in the traditional model was usually considered cheating. Today we understand that learners construct knowledge through social interaction. Teachers create assignments that engage students in working on a project within a small group. There are different levels of interaction within these groups depending on the way their task was established by the teacher. At a low level of interaction, students can be a part of a group yet work independently, participating in little collective knowledge construction. A higher level of interaction occurs when the members of the group share information, collectively develop new understandings through synthesis and synergy, and communicate that new knowledge, showing a transformation in their thinking.

Inquiry As Process

Students in a traditional classroom have little reason to gather and use information because most of their information is provided through textbooks and lectures. Although students do write papers in the traditional mode, more often these fall in the realm of regurgitation of facts. Since these research assignments tend to be teacher-led, students are often given requirements regarding the resources they may use for the paper. For example, they might be required to use a minimum number of books, magazines, and other resources. This requirement does expose students to a variety of resources, but it also inhibits their ability to learn to select resources independently.

In a more contemporary mode, students are encouraged to engage in a variety of projects; use multiple resources; and begin the process of finding, evaluating, and using information to construct new knowledge. As both teachers and students become more adept at inquiry and using a process model like Pathways to Knowledge, their experiences over time will lead them to a more independent application of process. The ultimate goal is for students to be able to demonstrate an exemplary level in the information literacy standards.

Applying the Rubric to Change

As you use the rubric in Figure 5.1 to plan change in your classroom, school, or school district, keep in mind that changing curriculum design and instructional practice in one or two indicators might be sufficient. For example, you might decide to change a unit to incorporate more critical thinking and the introduction of the Pathways model. When the unit is completed, evaluate the outcome and recommend changes that might be appropriate the next time the unit is taught. When planning begins for a second unit, you might think about adding one more change; for example, learner choice. This makes the change process more gradual, and all who are involved in the change can adapt with perhaps less stress. Remember that students will have new roles as well as teachers.

CHANGING LEARNING ENVIRONMENTS

Technology has brought great change to the learning environment in schools and beyond, into the learning neighborhood. Many educators, parents, and community leaders expected that technology would make a positive difference in schools by itself, but that has not happened. The presence of technology without a change in both curriculum design and instructional practice has only a limited impact on student achievement. Following is a profile of what a technology-rich learning environment might look like.

- ◆ Computer workstations are available for learner use throughout the school, in classrooms, labs, library media center, study areas, etc.

- ◆ Individual computers (e.g., notebooks, word processors, etc.) are available for personal learner or teacher use when needed.

- ◆ Learners and teachers have flexible access to computers for individual or small group use.

♦ An array of information tools are available that appropriately reflects the needs of learners and the curriculum (e.g., LMC electronic catalog, databases, indexes, bibliographies, etc.).

♦ Information resources are available that appropriately reflect the needs of learners and the curriculum (e.g., books, periodicals, references sources, and nonfiction, etc.) in all formats (i.e., print, electronic, and multimedia).

♦ Internet access is available from all areas of the neighborhood (e.g., classrooms, the library media center, homes, etc.).

♦ Visual and audio hardware that enables use of technology by large groups is available.

♦ Professionals staff the library media center and computer labs (i.e., LMS and technology specialists) and these educators work collaboratively with teachers and learners to enable the integration of technology across the curriculum.

♦ Technicians are available to maintain and repair hardware and software.

♦ Individualized professional development is required of all professional staff.

♦ Technology mini-courses are offered throughout the calendar year for all members of the neighborhood.

♦ Selection policies reflect the need for all learning resources (e.g., print, electronic, multimedia, etc.) to support the curricular needs of all learners in the neighborhood.

♦ An acceptable use policy (AUP) is in place that enables information access relevant to the curricular needs of learners and requires responsible use of technology by all learners.

♦ A technology planning process is in place that is ongoing and involves the input from all members of the learning neighborhood. (Pappas, 1999, p. 27)

THE CHANGE PROCESS

In Scenario 5.1, Dr. Henderson had already determined that there was a need to integrate a process model into the middle school social studies curriculum. At her meeting with the social studies teachers she was not met with a great deal of enthusiasm. The problem? She was already at the "Pilot some possibilities" step of the Fostering Systemic Change process shown in Figure 5.2. She had skipped over three steps in this change process and failed to recognize that the common strategies in the middle of the model were important to her goals. She had not communicated with any of the social studies teachers or the library media specialist before the meeting, which had a negative impact on strategies

Figure 5.2. Fostering Systemic Change. ©2002 Pappas and Tepe.

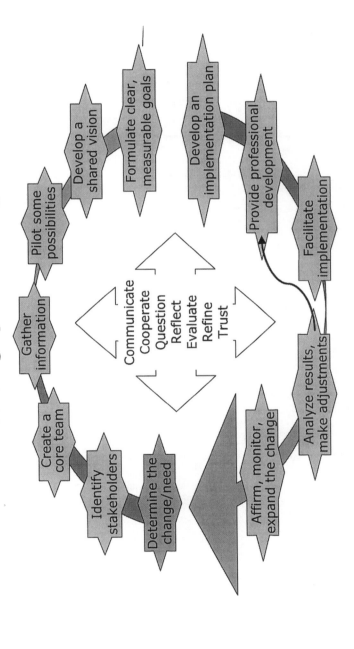

Fostering Systemic Change

Develop a shared vision
Formulate clear, measurable goals
Develop an implementation plan
Provide professional development
Facilitate implementation
Analyze results, make adjustments
Affirm, monitor, expand the change
Determine the change/need
Identify stakeholders
Create a core team
Gather information
Pilot some possibilities

Communicate
Cooperate
Question
Reflect
Evaluate
Refine
Trust

Creating the Climate for Sustainable Change

Administration Must...

➤ Empower and encourage stakeholders.
➤ Legitimize the effort through support, acknowledgment, and communication.
➤ Support the change effort verbally, in writing, and in actions.
➤ Empower the core team.
➤ Provide resources, time, and budget.
➤ Understand the time and determination needed for systemic change.

Fundamental Principles

Support risk-taking.
Promote inquiry.
Encourage questioning.
Consider timing.
Learn to listen.
Build/use communication strategies.
Practice ethical behavior.

Core Team Must...

➤ Manage the process.
➤ Develop a holistic perspective.
➤ Develop consensus-building skills.
➤ Foster teamwork, manage disagreement.
➤ Acknowledge resistance and use it to improve project.
➤ Be sensitive to needs and emotions of individuals
➤ Be sure desired goals fit culture.
➤ Celebrate successes.

like trust and cooperation. Dr. Henderson now has a problem. There is the possibility that Craig Williams, the LMS, might have saved the situation with his suggestion to visit another middle school where Pathways is being used. Craig is in the Gather Information stage of the model, but the situation is still a bit tenuous.

How might Dr. Henderson have changed her approach? She knows that the new social studies curriculum focuses on process, critical thinking, and inquiry learning, and that is a change from the previous curriculum document. Let's re-create this scenario and assume that she recently purchased a copy of this book, so she can apply the Fostering Systemic Change (Figure 5.2) model and use the Fostering Systemic Change: Advance Organizer (see Appendix E).

SCENARIO 5.1 (cont.)

Dr. Henderson skims through the Advance Organizer and notices that the same strategies that appeared on the model are also listed in a small diamond insert at the top of each page. These strategies are Communicate, Cooperate, Question, Reflect, Evaluate, Refine, and Trust. By inference, these all have relevance to each stage of the change process. She also notices the information across the bottom of the model, with the heading "Creating the Climate for Sustainable Change." These are responsibilities for both administrators and a core team, with fundamental principles that relate to both groups. As she looks over the list, she realizes that she has already violated the "Consider timing" and "Learn to listen" principles.

Dr. Henderson returns to the Advance Organizer and the Identify Stakeholders stage. She decides to have a conversation with several teachers and principals to determine the stakeholders and to create a core team.

At the first meeting of the core team she gives them copies of the Fostering Systemic Change model and the Advance Organizer and asks them if they would be interested in using this process as a means of initiating change. The core team agrees. Craig Williams, the library media specialist who helped her initially, asks the group how they want to proceed with gathering information. Two teachers who were part of the group that visited the Silver Creek Middle School share the information gathered during that trip. The group talks about contacting other educators who are using the Pathways model with inquiry learning. Craig volunteers to do a literature search. Dr. Henderson reminds them of the common strategies related to the model and suggests that they each keep a journal of reflections during the change process. Another member of the core team encourages the group to keep a list of questions they have about this change they are considering.

In subsequent meetings the core team identifies several possibilities for pilot projects and establishes short-term goals and evaluation strategies to determine the results of the pilots. Members of the core team decide they want to have opportunities to visit and observe in these pilot sites. They agree to ask the teachers involved to keep journals of their reflections during the pilot and to share a summary of the reflections with the core team when the pilot is concluded. They also ask that each teacher keep a selection of student projects to share with the team.

The results of the pilot projects and their information gathering help the team decide to try several process models before they make a decision to adopt one specific model. They talk about who should make the decision about which model to use. Craig suggests they take several models back with them and actually pursue a research activity with one or two of them. Team members spend time with the teachers and some students who have participated in the pilot projects. The core team uses the input to help them make decisions about an implementation plan and professional development. The core team agrees on the adoption of a process model and goals and milestones to use for the implementation plan. They decide to implement the plan in the fall of the next school year, several months away.

The core team agrees to work together another year to analyze the results of the new program and help make adjustments in the plan when needed. They understand that change will be a challenge for some teachers and administrators and agree to act as mentors for those who want that type of support.

Dr. Henderson and the core team follow the Fostering Systemic Change process and meet late in the fall after the implementation plan has been in place for several months. The purpose of this meeting is to evaluate the process they have used to initiate change. They want to know what changes they might make in the process as additional core teams are established when another need to change occurs.

The Fundamental Principles and the responsibilities of the core team and administration are important if change is to become systemic and sustainable. Your application of the Fostering Systemic Change process might be different from the experiences of Dr. Henderson and the core team. Many variables will have an impact on change in your district that may not have been in effect in this fictitious scenario.

CONCLUSION

The scenario in this chapter shows a change process at the district level, but we encourage those who see issues or problems and want to initiate change to understand that change can start with one person in the classroom, library media center, or district office. Change is needed. Education is at a crossroads in this country, and the profession needs individuals willing to challenge the status quo and propose new ideas and ways of doing things. The adage, "this works, why change it" represents the ostrich approach to life. There are too many educators today with their heads buried in the sand. We encourage you to be change agents. However, always remember that change takes time, so don't be impatient, and do plan well. You can always find ways to try an innovative idea with another individual, but if you want that idea to grow beyond that initial experience you must have advocates and a plan for change.

We want to leave you with one last thought. Change, exciting change, is happening in schools across the country. We encourage you to find places and people who are also interested in change. Network with them and learn from each other. One place to start is the Society for Organizational Learning (SOL) at http://www.solonline.org/.

Dan Baron said it well:

> Change will happen regardless of our fondest desires to simply let it flow around us. Like a wave coming on shore, we sometimes can stand still and let the water go around us, but as it recedes it will leach the sand from around our feet, and sometimes it may have the power to drag us into its belly. As long as we are active professionals, we are obligated not only to deal effectively with the rapid

change that is readily apparent all around us, but also actively to be a part of guiding the change process. The latter fulfills our leadership responsibilities . . . [presented in *Information Power*]. (2001, p. 49)

REFERENCES

Baron, D. (2001, March). Beyond March madness: An Update on change and the school library media specialist. *School Library Media Activities Monthly 17* (7), 49–51.

Donham, J. (1998). *Assessment of information processes and products.* [Booklet]. McHenry, IL: Follett Software Co.

Pappas, Marjorie L. (1999). Changing learning and libraries in schools. *School Library Media Activities Monthly 16* (1), 26–29, 32.

Pathways to Knowledge® Model

Figure A.1. Pathways to Knowledge®.

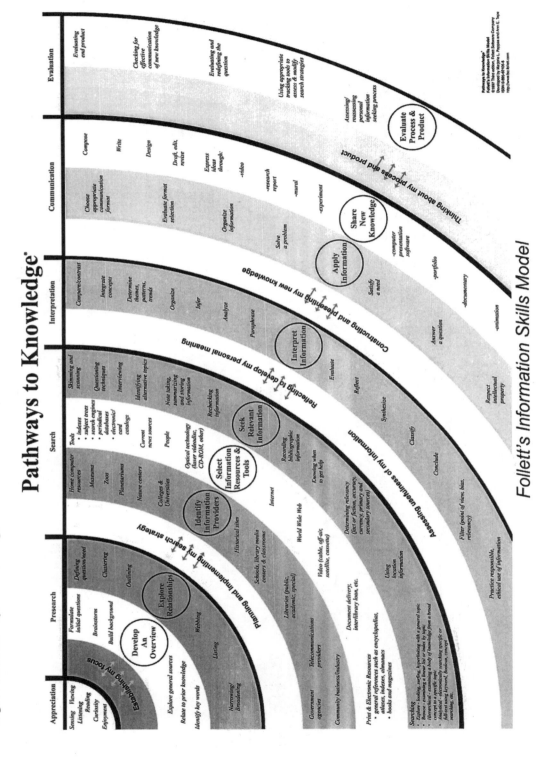

Follett Software Company is the copyright owner of the Pathways to Knowledge® Model, Extended Text Version and Introduction materials associated with the Pathways to Knowledge Model. These materials are used with the permission of Follett Software Company and may not be reproduced in any form without written permission from the Follett Software Company.

Figure A.2. Pathways—Extended Text Version.

Pathways to Knowledge®—Extended Text Version

I. Appreciation

Individuals appreciate literature, the arts, nature and information in the world around them through varied and multiple formats, including stories, film, paintings, natural settings, music, books, periodicals, the Web, video, etc. Appreciation often fosters curiosity and imagination, which can be a prelude to a discovery phase in an information seeking activity. As learners proceed through the stages of information seeking their appreciation grows and matures throughout the process.

Function: Not Applicable
General Strategies: Not Applicable
Specific Strategies include:

> listening
>
> sensing
>
> curiosity
>
> imagining
>
> viewing
>
> reading
>
> creating
>
> writing
>
> discussing
>
> verbalizing
>
> appreciating
>
> enjoying
>
> evaluating

II. Presearch

The Presearch stage enables searchers to make a connection between their topic and prior knowledge. They may begin by brainstorming a web or questions that focus on what they know about their topic and what they want to know. This process may require them to engage in exploratory searching through general sources to develop a broad overview of their topic and explore the relationships among subtopics. Presearch provides searchers with strategies to narrow their focus and develop specific questions or define information needs.

Function: Establishing My Focus
General Strategies: Develop an Overview
　　　　　　　　　　Explore Relationships
Specific Strategies include:

> building background information
>
> exploring general sources of information

(Figure A.2 continues on page 108.)

Figure A.2 (*continues*)

relating information to prior knowledge

formulating initial questions

identifying keywords

brainstorming ideas and information about topic

relating topics and concepts through webbing, outlining, clustering, etc.

narrowing or broadening a topic

developing specific research questions

defining information needs

following procedures for using information technologies and facilities

seeking help from appropriate sources when needed

evaluating the outcome of Presearch

III. Search

During the Search stage, searchers identify appropriate information providers, resources and tools, then plan and implement a search strategy to find information relevant to their research question or information need. Searchers are open to using print and electronic tools and resources, cooperative searching and interaction with experts.

Function: Planning & Implementing My Search Strategy

General Strategies: Identify Information Providers

Select Information Resources & Tools

Seek Relevant Information

Specific Strategies include:

applying resource location skills

asking questions to clarify meaning

distinguishing among information sources

using information sources appropriately

recording appropriate information through summarizing, quoting and listing significant facts (handwritten and/or electronic)

recording bibliographic information

gathering information from authentic and human resources

selecting and using information tools (e.g., indexes, catalogs, bibliographies, directories, search engines)

developing search strategies for print and electronic resources, including

Explore Search (looking, surfing, hyperlinking with a general topic)

Browse Search (examining a linear list or index by topic)

Hierarchical Search (examining a body of knowledge from a broad concept to a specific topic)

Analytical Search (electronically searching specified or full text using keyword, Boolean, concept searching, etc.)

understanding the concept of linear (print) and nonlinear (electronic) organization of information

skimming and scanning to gather information

determining relevancy of information— fact or fiction, accuracy, currency, primary and secondary sources, and relevancy to research question or information need

evaluating the appropriateness of information providers, tools, and resources

evaluating the results of the search strategy

IV. Interpretation

Information requires interpretation to become knowledge. The Interpretation stage engages searchers in the process of analyzing, synthesizing and evaluating information to determine its relevancy and usefulness to their research question or information need. Throughout this stage searchers reflect on the information they have gathered and construct personal meaning.

Function: Assessing Usefulness of My Information

Reflecting to Develop My Personal Meaning

General Strategies: Interpret Information

Specific Strategies include:

inferring

drawing conclusions

paraphrasing

filtering information (point of view, bias, etc.)

reflecting

organizing information

practicing responsible and ethical use of information

comparing and contrasting

analyzing

determining credibility

classifying

evaluating information

understanding cause and effect

integrating concepts

synthesizing

determining themes, patterns, trends

evaluating information to support or refute a problem, or research question

(Figure A.2 continues on page 110.)

Figure A.2 (*continues*)

V. Communication

The Communication stage allows searchers to organize, apply, and present new knowledge relevant to their research question or information need. They choose a format that appropriately reflects the new knowledge they need to convey, then plan and create their product.

Function: Constructing & Presenting My New Knowledge

General Strategies Apply Information
                       Share New Knowledge

Specific Strategies include:

       organizing information

       selecting an appropriate communication format

       applying information to answer a question or solve a problem

       expressing creative ideas through creating, speaking, composing, writing, designing, etc.

       developing a draft or initial version, editing, and revising

       evaluating the format selection

       presenting new knowledge through selected formats

       respecting intellectual property

The communication formats below are a representative sample and are not meant to be an all-inclusive list. Some formats are relevant to more than one category and are listed under all that apply. For example, demonstration is listed under both audio and visual. The visual category includes both static and motion visuals. Multimedia is defined as two or more formats. Formats include:

Visual	**Visual/Motion**	**Text**	**Multimedia**
diagram	TV documentary	research paper	sound/slide show
timeline	video tape	writing a book	presentation software
model	animation	book report	exhibit
Venn diagram	video conferencing	crossword puzzle	computer program
slide show	film	journal	portfolio
puppet show		creative writing	Web page
poster		letter writing	
diorama		word find	
transparency	**Oral**	computer program	
art work	panel discussion	newspaper	
graph	music	puzzle	
chart	demonstration	portfolio	
presentation software	travelogue	report	
book jacket	interview	database	
computer program	speech	spreadsheet	
puzzle	debate	story	

Visual	**Oral**	**Text**
display	skit or play	biography
mural	dialog	
map	story	
graphic		
exhibit		
photograph		
bulletin board		
drawing		
Web page		

VI. Evaluation

Evaluation (self and peer) is ongoing in this nonlinear information process model and should occur throughout each stage. Searchers use their evaluation of the process to make revisions that enable them to develop their own unique information seeking process. It is through this continuous evaluation and revision process that searchers develop the ability to become independent searchers. Searchers also evaluate their product or the results of their communication of new knowledge.

Function: Thinking About My Process & Product

General Strategies: Evaluate Process & Product

Specific Strategies include:

     evaluating and redefining the question

     assessing/reassessing personal information seeking process

     evaluating end product

     checking for effective communication of new knowledge

     using appropriate tracking tools (e.g., logs, journals) to assess and modify search strategies

Figure A.3. Pathways to Knowledge® (Blank).

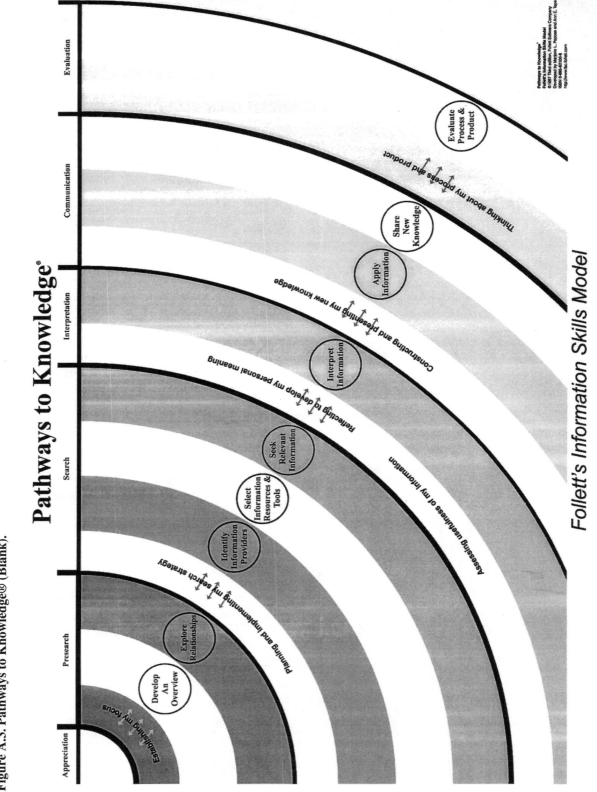

Heroes Planning Guide and Presentation Rubric

Figure B.1. Heroes Planning Guide.

Heroes Planning Guide

Level: Middle School   Subject(s): Eng/LA

Topic: Heroes

Essential Questions

How do heroes influence my life?

What characteristics do heroes possess in common?

Inquiry Instructional Strategies

Engagement, Questioning, and Knowledge Construction:

Pathways Model Instruction:

Students use an inquiry process that shows their ability to be independent learners. This inquiry process includes relating to prior knowledge, establishing appropriate questions, engaging in a questioning process, using appropriate resources to gather information, evaluating information for appropriateness, constructing new understandings, and communicating their findings.

> **Curriculum Connection**
>
> **Illinois Learning Standards [http://www.isbe.state.il.us/ils/lst andards.html]**
>
> English/ LA: Goal 4 (Listening & Speaking) Listen and speak effectively in a variety of situations.
>
> English/LA: Goal 5 (Research), Use LA to acquire, assess, and communicate information.

Students are:

New Users	Novice Users	Proficient Users	Independent Users
		X	

Pathways model strategies to be taught in this unit:

Apprecia-tion	Presearch	Search	Interpreta-tion	Communica-tion	Evaluation
	Webbing (review)	Analytical searching (review)	Synthesis Reflection	Create a *HyperStudio* and *PowerPoint* presentation	Self-evaluation of presenta-tion using a rubric

Assessment

Criteria:

Use questions and reflection as they gather and use information (process)

Develop and apply an information-gathering plan (process)

Evaluate information for relevance, scope, and accuracy (process)

Organize information to show patterns (process)

Choose an appropriate format for presenting information (process)

Apply new understandings of hero characteristics to a presentation about one hero (product)

Self-evaluate presentation based on rubric assessment criteria (product)

Strategies:

Journals, small group logs, presentation rubric

Construct a common set of hero characteristics collaboratively through consensus

Demonstrate new understanding of hero characteristics as these apply to self through a reflective writing

(Figure B-1 continues on page 116.)

Figure B.1 (*continues*)

Unit Schedule

Day	Teacher	Library Media Specialist	Students
1	Opens the unit with a special program that includes guests from the local university, including several students who are successful athletes, both male and female. The guests have been asked to talk a short time about their lives and what has happened along the way to help them be successful.		Engage in a conversation with guests.
2	This first session is held in the LMC. With LMS, facilitates the session. Posts the essential understanding, the question, and the content understandings on large poster paper so all students can read this information. With LMS, engages students in a brainstorming discussion about their heroes. As a large group they identify heroes and construct a web that categorizes their heroes by profession or relationship to individual students, using large paper. For example, a hero might be a mother or father. Asks, "What would you like to know about heroes?" and "How would you like to pursue this inquiry?"	Asks students where they might find information about people who might be heroes. Students suggest talking with local people (i.e. musicians, sports figures, etc.), using encyclopedias, almanacs, subject specific encyclopedias. Online: *Wilson Biographies Plus, Middle Search Plus,* and *Elibrary.* The LMS reminds them that *Yahoo* might be helpful under People. Also *Biography.com.*	Engage in a brainstorming session about heroes. After some discussion, students decide they need more information about various heroes before they can develop any further plans. Their web includes categories of heroes (e.g. athletes, local people, family members, musicians, actors). They decide to work in groups to gather information about other people who might be heroes. They spend the next two days in the LMC gathering information.

3–4	Works with the LMS in the LMC to facilitate gathering information. At the end of each class period, poses a question and asks students to write in their journals. For example, "What was the most significant thing you learned today?" or "How did the information you gathered today change your thinking about heroes?"	Works with the teacher to facilitate gathering information.	Work in small groups to gather information. At the end of the class period, spend five minutes writing in their journals.
5	Engages students in another brainstorming session where they add to the original class web about heroes. Asks students, "what is your next step?" With LMS, reads and assesses journals	With teacher, reads and assesses journals.	Engage in developing the class web about heroes using the additional information they have gathered. In discussion they all seem to have heroes who are local and those who are famous outside their community. They decide that each of them will find more in-depth information about two individual heroes. Much discussion centers on what they want to know about these people. Finally agree on the following research questions: 1) Who are these people and what has made them famous? 2) What (if any) life-changing events occurred in the lives of these people? 3) How were the lives of these two people similar and different?

(Figure B.1 continues on page 118.)

Figure B.1 (*continues*)			Develop a list of characteristics about their individual heroes. As a small group they discuss these characteristics and agree on a composite set of characteristics for the group's heroes. When this is completed, they meet again as a large group and discuss these composite lists of characteristics. The class reaches consensus on a list of characteristics that all heroes seem to have in common. Also decide they want an opportunity to share one of their heroes with the class. The format for this presentation includes some visual representations of the hereo.
6-10	Facilitates and coaches as students work in groups to gather information. Provides mini-lessons on using a T chart for recording information, bibliographic format, and strategies for interpreting their information. Meets with small groups periodically to foster discussion about the characteristic list they are developing. Encourages them to question their new information and use this questioning process to make decisions about further research. Engages students in writing in their journals on a daily basis by providing questions for prompted writing that focus on both content and process.	Facilitates and coaches as students work in groups to gather information. Provides mini-lessons on keyword searching; evaluating information for relevance, accuracy, bias, and currency, use of grphic organizers; and capturing pictures for use in their presentations, as needed. Meets with small groups periodically to foster discussion about the process they are using to gather and use information. Encourages them to question their new information and use this questioning process to make decisions about further research.	Work in collaborative groups to gather information about their heroes. Record the information they have gathered using a T chart that allows them to summarize new information on one side and reflect on that information on the other side. Use graphic organizers (e.g. Time lines, Venn diagrams, and story boards) to record and interpret their new information. Meet in small groups to discuss their list of hero characteristics.

		Engages students in writing in their journals by providing questions for prompted writing that focus on their process. With teacher, reads and assess journals.	
11-15	Facilitates small group and full class discussions to enable students to reach consensus on a composite list of hero characteristics. Holds mini-lessons on developing a storyboard for visual presentations. With LMS, reads and assesses journals. Facilitates discussion with students to develop a rubric that will be used to assess their presentations.	With technology coordinator (TC), teaches mini-lessons on *PowerPoint* and *HyperStudio* programs for those students who want to use these programs for their visual presentations. With teacher, reads and assesses journals.	Meet in small groups and then with the full class to reach consensus on a composite list of hero characteristics. Work on presentations comparing their hero to the composite list of common hero characteristics. Write invitations to parents and selected community people to come to their presentations on heroes. Work with teacher to develop a rubric that will be used to assess their presentations, both by the teacher and as a peer- and self-assessment.
16-17	With LMS and TC, coaches and facilitates as students complete presentations.	With teacher and TC, coaches and facilitates as students complete presentations.	Complete presentations. Several students work on a visual that shows their composite list of common characteristics for heroes to be displayed in their classroom.
18-19	Facilitates presentation events. Assesses presentations using the presentation rubric.	Is available (as well as TC) to trouble shoot if needed.	Give presentations. Use presentation rubric for peer- and self-assessment.

(Figure B.1 continues on page 120.)

Figure B.1 (*continues*)

20	Engages students in a final prompted writing on the question, "How do heroes influence my life?"		Write in journals to respond to the question, "How do heroes influence my life?"
21-23	With LMS, reads and assesses journals. Meets with LMS and TC to evaluate the unit.	With teacher, reads and assesses journals.	

Collaboration Notes

Teacher and library media specialist (LMS) met for a planning session to develop the Unit Planning Guide. They made decisions about teaching and facilitating responsibilities and decided they needed to ask the technology coordinator to join them for part of this unit.

Several short meetings were held during the unit to make adjustments in the schedule to reflect student needs.

The LMS, teacher, and technology coordinator used e-mail to resolve daily issues.

The LMS, teacher, and technology coordinator met after the unit was concluded for an evaluation discussion about the unit.

Resources

Note: All Web addresses accessed December 21, 2001.

Biography.com. (2001). A&E Television Networks. [Online]. Available: http://www .biography.com/

Britannica.com. (2001). [Online]. Available: http://www.britannica.com/

Electric Library. (2001). Infonautics. [Online]. Available: http://ask.elibrary.com/

HyperStudio®. (2001). Knowledge Adventure.

Illinois Learning Standards. English/Language Arts Standards. Research Goal. (2001). Illinois State Board of Education. [Online]. Available: http://www.isbe .state.il.us/ils/english/english.html

Middle Search Plus. (n.d.). EBSCO. [Online]. Available: http://www.epnet.com/

PowerPoint®. (2001). Microsoft.

Wilson Biographies Plus. (2001). H. W. Wilson. [Online]. Available: http://www.hwwilson.com/Databases/biosplusi.htm

Yahoo. (2001). [Online]. Available: http://www.yahoo.com/

<u>General Resources</u>

Various search engines

Storyboard framework

Graphic organizers (e.g., timeline, T chart, comparison chart, Venn diagram)

Electronic encyclopedias

©2002 Pappas and Tepe

Figure B.2. Heroes Presentation Rubric.

Indicators	Novice	Proficient	Expert
Organization	Irregular sequence.	Logical sequence.	Logical and interesting sequence.
Hero Content	Content omits important elements of personal hero's life.	Content conveys essential information about personal hero.	Content appropriately elaborates beyond essential information about personal hero.
Hero Characteristics	Little or no comparison apparent between hero characteristics and personal hero.	Makes effective comparisons between hero characteristics and personal hero.	Shows understanding of relationship between hero characteristics and life of personal hero.
Presentation Mode	Mode is inappropriate for knowledge being presented and presentation skills.	Selects an appropriate mode for skill level; mode matches knowledge of topic.	Selection of mode significantly enhances presentation.
Presentation Skills	Makes little eye contact, lacks enthusiasm, and fails to use resources where appropriate.	Makes eye contact; shows enthusiasm for subject; appropriately incorporates resources when needed.	Engages and involves audience in presentation; selection and use of resources enhances delivery.

© 2002 Pappas and Tepe

Whales
Planning Guide
and
Pathways Model

Figure C.1. Whales Planning Guide.
©2002 Pappas and Tepe

Whales Planning Guide

Level: 5   Subject(s): Science

Topic: Whales

Essential Questions

How do whales live?

How do whales migrate?

Why are whales endangered?

Curriculum Connection

Illinois Learning Standards
[http://www.isbe.state.il.us/ils/lstandards.html]

Science: Goal 12 (Concepts & Principles), B, Late Elementary

English/Language Arts: Goal 5 (Research), A-C, Late Elementary

Instructional Strategies

Engagement, Questioning, and Knowledge Construction:

Show a clip from a video about whales. Ask students what questions they have about whales.

Pathways Model Instruction:

Students are:

New Users	Novice Users	Proficient Users	Independent Users
X			

Pathways model strategies to be taught in this unit:

Apprecia-tion	Presearch	Search	Interpre-tation	Communica-tion	Evaluation
	Brainstorm Define Question	Use a subject tree, catalog, and WWW	Organize, evaluate	Create a mural	Use rubric for self-evaluation

Assessment

Criteria:

Content: Students will apply their knowledge of whale life to show an understanding of migration patterns and different perspectives on their endangered status.

Process: Students will reflect on the process followed in the Pathways model through small and large group discussions.

Strategies:

Students will construct a wall mural showing the habitat of whales in a specific oceanic region and their migration patterns.

Students will develop a presentation about their mural that explains migration patterns and causes of whales' endangered status.

Unit Schedule

Day	Teacher	Library Media Specialist	Students
1	Shows a short clip from *In the Company of Whales* video. (Engagement & Appreciation) Engages students in a follow-up discussion by asking the question, "What did you see in this video that arouses your curiosity?" Records their comments and questions on chart paper.		Watch the *Whales* video and respond to the teacher's question.

(Figure C.1 continues on page 126.)

Figure C.1 (*continues*)

2	Focuses on brainstorming. With LMS, models a brainstorming activity on a topic that would engage the interest of students, e.g., popular music, amusement parks, or video games. When finished, engages the students in a "what happened here?" conversation, leading them into an understanding of the brainstorming process. With LMS, engages students in a brainstorming session using a KWL chart.	Does same as teacher.	Watch the brainstorming between teacher and LMS.
3	Tapes a large world map (laminated) up on a wall in the LMC and provides washable transparency pens for student use. Shortly before the end of this class period, asks students to look at the map and asks, "What questions do you have about the information you have gathered?" One of the patterns that should emerge is that whales travel around the ocean. They do not live in the same part of the ocean at all times of the year.	One of the major questions on the KWL chart under "What do I want to know" is: Where do whales live? Talks with students about gathering general background information. Guides them to general and science encyclopedias and suggests they look for information that might answer that question.	Look for general information in response to the question, "Where do whales live?" As they gather information about specific whales. they write the name of the whale in the part of the ocean where it lives.
4	Engages students in a discussion about how they might pursue their study of whale life and their migration patterns.	Provides students with blank copies of the Pathways Model. Asks students to work in small groups to plan their research process. After a short time, asks groups to share their plans with the class.	Work in small groups to plan their research process. Decide to work in small groups to explore the whale population that inhabits regions of the oceans and the impact of migration on those regions. Student groups develop their research questions.

| 5–7 | Goes with students to the LMC and helps to facilitate their information search process. Talks about note taking. Has set up small pieces of paper in different colors. (Note: use colored paper and cut in one-quarter-inch pieces.) A different color is designated for each type of whale. At the end of each class teacher asks students to meet in their small groups and respond to the questions:

1) What are the most important things you learned about whales today?

2) What new whale species did you find that live in and/or migrate to your section of the ocean?

As new whale species are discovered, new colors are assigned for note taking. | Asks students where they might find information about whale habitats. Students brainstorm a list of possible resources including the Internet. Shows students how to use *Yahooligans* (directory) and *KidsClick* (search engine). Suggests students use the catalog to find books and *Middle Search Plus* for magazine articles. Shows students how to find Web sites using the established Favorites file on Whales.

Near the end of day 7, meets with each small group, asking them to focus on the way they gathered information. For example, the LMS might ask the following questions:

1) What are some resources you used?

2) Which resources seemed to have the best information?

3) What were some frustrations you experienced?

Meets with small groups to refocus them on their Pathways research plan using the blank Pathways model. | Gather information based on their research questions. Brainstorm a list of keywords to use as they search in the catalog and periodical database. As they gather information they take notes on colored pieces of paper, using a different color for each species of whale. At the end of each class period, student groups summarize their information and post this summary in the region of the ocean they are studying.

Revisit their research plan periodically to check for next steps and perhaps make revisions. |

(Figure C.1 continues on page 128.)

Figure C-1 (*continues*)

8-9	Gives students a graphic organizer for classifying. Asks students to record information about each species of whale based on their research questions, (e.g., what do whales eat, how do they communicate, regions they migrate to, when they migrate). Asks students to examine the map for common patterns: for example, what are some similarities or differences in the way whales migrate? What are some unique characteristics of whales that live primarily in different oceanic regions?	Meets with student groups as they organize their information. Asks them questions like these: 1) How do you know your information is accurate? 2) Does the information you gathered answer your original research questions? If the answer to the second question is "no," then the LMS guides them to finding additional information.	Create summary of information by whale species and post these sheets on the map in the regions where the whales live. Create a mind map that starts with the various oceanic regions they are studying. Create this mind map using a large sheet of bulletin board paper taped to a wall of the classroom. As they identify relationships between specific whales living in different regions, they draw dotted lines to make a connection.
10–12	Provides large sheets of bulletin board paper for students to use to create their murals.		Work on their murals. Begin by drawing the major coastal regions contiguous to their oceanic region. Murals depict types of whales that live in the region, family life, feeding patterns, habitat characteristics, and migration patterns by season.
13–14	Asks students to select one type of whale from their region and develop a presentation showing how these whales migrate throughout the year and the interaction with people that causes the endangered status of whales.	Assists students.	To complete this project, some students return to the LMC to gather additional information. Work on presentations and present these to the other students in their class.

| 15 | With LMS, meets with students to discuss the Pathways process they followed in this inquiry project. Begins the discussion with a large poster of Pathways that includes only the stages across the top and the various bands. Then asks students to think back through the steps of their project using the blank Pathways organizer they developed as a research plan. Asks questions such as, "What did you do first? What was the next thing you did?" As students talk, the LMS records their process on the Pathways poster using the Pathways strategy names. The LMS and teacher insert strategies students miss until they have their research on the model. Then the LMS and teacher pose some process evaluation questions: What were some frustrations? What might you do differently next time? | Does same as teacher. | Look back over the process they followed to gather, evaluate, and use information for this project. In small groups use the research plan they developed early in the unit (i.e., the blank version of Pathways). As a large group, consider the strategies that worked the best for them, frustrations they encountered, and possible changes in the process for the future. |

Collaboration Notes

Teacher and LMS met several weeks ahead of the start of the unit to plan the unit. They talked about the writing, science, and information literacy concepts and standards they wanted to cover in the unit and developed the essential questions. The LMS did some research in sources of information and developed a list of Web sites that were saved into a Favorites file on the library media center's network.

Another meeting was held several days before the unit was started, just to be sure all details were in place.

In between meetings and throughout the unit, the teacher and LMS exchanged e-mail messages as the need arose to ask questions or deal with problems.

They held short meetings prior to several class sessions where they needed to work together with students, e.g., the searching sessions in the LMC or the sessions that focused on organizing and evaluating information.

When the unit was completed, the LMS and teacher met to evaluate the unit and the process they had followed to create the unit.

Resources

Note: All Web addresses accessed December 21, 2001.

In the Company of Whales. [Video]. Discovery. 90 minutes. Order at: http://www
.discovery.com

Secrets of the Humpback. [Video]. Discovery. 50 minutes. Order at: http://www
.discovery.com

Whales. National Wildlife Federation. [Video]. Filmed in IMAX®. Narrated by
Patrick Stewart. Order at: http://www.nwf.org/productions/whales.html.

Web Resources

Note: All Web addresses accessed December 21, 2001.

All About Whales. (1998–2001). EnchantedLearning.com. [Online]. Available:
http://www.enchantedlearning.com/subjects/whales/allabout/

Animal Information Database. SeaWorld. (2001). Busch Entertainment. [On-
line]. Available: http://www.seaworld.org/infobook.html

Encarta. (2001). Microsoft. [Online]. Available: http://encarta.msn.com/default
.asp?

KidsClick! (2000). Colorado State Library/ACLIN. [Online]. Available:
http://www.kidsclick.org/
Note: Search under "whales."

The Majestic Presence of the Whale. (1995–2001). ThinkQuest. [Online]. Available: http://library.thinkquest.org/2605/

Whale Watching Web. (2001). WWW Virtual Library. [Online]. Available:
http://www.physics.helsinki.fi/whale/#World

WhaleNet. (2000). J. Michael Williamson. [Online]. Available: http://whale
.wheelock.edu/

Whales Online. (n.d.). Natural Heritage Trust. [Online]. Available:
http://www.whales-online.org/

Yahooligans. (2001). Yahoo. [Online] Available: http://www.yahoo.com/
Select: Science & Nature > Animals > Marine Life > Whales

Figure C.2. Pathways to Knowledge® (Simon's notes on Whales Unit).

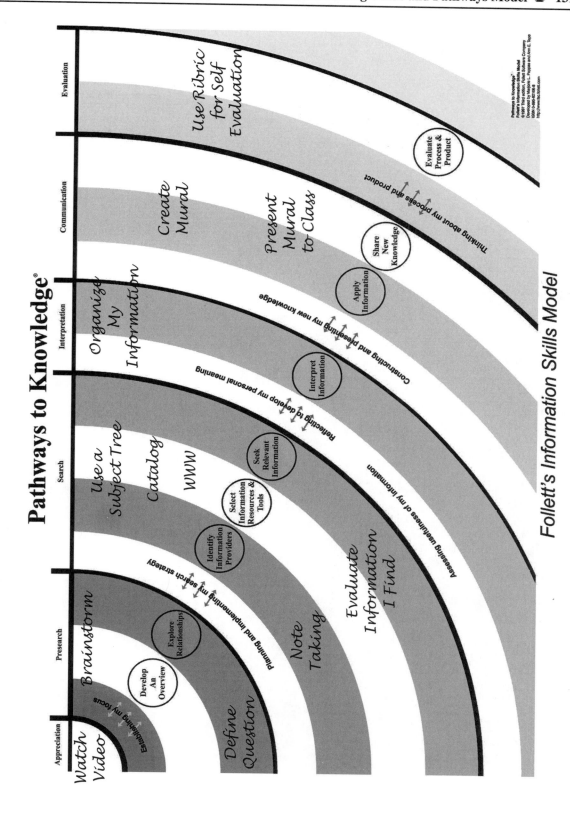

Native American Planning Guide

Figure D.1. Native American Planning Guide, page 134

Figure D.1. Native American Planning Guide. ©2002 Pappas and Tepe

Native American Planning Guide

Level: 10   **Subject(s): Eng/LA**

Topic: Native Americans

Essential Questions

How have biases and stereotypes been characterized in the arts, literature, and other types of media that represent Native Americans?

How does stereotyping affect prejudice and bias?

How have the lives of Native Americans been affected by the arts and news media?

Instructional Strategies

Engagement, Questioning, and Knowledge Construction:

Use a clip from an old western movie that includes scenes of American Indians and settlers.

Pathways Model Instruction:

Brainstorming to develop a mind map using *Inspiration*.

Review developing a research question.

Teach developing a research plan and a keyword list.

Review with students the use of periodical databases.

Teach evaluating information.

Review using a comparison chart graphic organizer.

Curriculum Connection

Illinois Learning Standards [http://www.isbe.state.il.us/ils/lstandards.html]

English/ LA: Goal 3 (Writing) Write to communicate for a variety of purposes.

English/LA: Goal 5 (Research) Use LA to acquire, assess, and communicate

Students are:

New Users	Novice Users	Proficient Users	Independent Users
	X		

Pathways model strategies to be taught in this unit:

Appreciation	Presearch	Search	Interpretation	Communication	Evaluation
Curiosity Discovery	Brain-storming Questioning	Develop a plan Search strategies Evaluate information	Compare Synthesize	Write a short story or diary	Reflect on process

Assessment

Criteria:

Change in personal perception of Native Americans.

Writing shows student's understanding of various perspectives relevant to the time period.

Writing is historically accurate, reflects appropriate historical context.

Strategies:

Writing project (e.g., short story, diary, magazine article).

Reflections that show changes in personal viewpoint.

Logs and reflections show Pathways model process followed and some growth in the use of specific strategies from previous application of Pathways.

Unit Schedule

Day	Teacher	Library Media Specialist	Students
1	Directs students to write first reflective entry in journal in response to the prompt: "What are some examples of Native American stereotyping?" Shows a video clip of an old western movie with a focus on the American Indian and settlers.		Write in journals in response to the writing prompt Discuss in small groups. Share information with large group.

(Figure D.1 continues on page 136.)

Figure D.1 (*continues*)

2	Posts the essential questions for the unit in the classroom where all can see. Assists LMS in facilitating the brainstorming session.	Gives students a copy of the Pathways model, reviews the stages, and highlights some of the strategies on which they will place special emphasis in this unit. Uses *Inspiration* software to lead a brainstorming session on stereotypes of Native Americans. Students are encouraged to use the essential questions as a catalyst for their brainstorming.	Participate in brainstorming session and construct the beginning part of a mind map.
3–5	Meets with students to assist as they make decisions about their research groups. Reviews the Writing Process with students, pointing to a poster on the bulletin board that includes the five-step process. —Prewriting —Drafting —Responding and Revising —Proofreading —Publishing Reviews the strategies of Prewriting. At the close of each class period, asks students to take out their journals and spend five minutes writing in response to prompts such as: 1) What were the most important things you learned today? 2) How might this affect what you do tomorrow? 3) What did you learn today that surprised you?	Helps students gather background information on stereotypes of Native Americans. Provides each student group with a copy of the mind map constructed using *Inspiration.* Tells students to check back if they need more instruction in using *Inspiration* as they continue to build their mind maps.	Make decisions about their research groups using the major clusters on the mind map. Each research group (4–6 students) develops initial questions to use as they gather background information. As they gather background information, they add to the original mind map. Make daily entries in their journals, reflecting on process.

	4) Which Presearch strategy did you use today? 5) How did this strategy help you add to your mind map?		
6–8	Meets with each research group. Instructs groups to select a stereotyping source (film, stories, newspapers, etc.) and develop research questions based on the information in their mind map. Students are instructed to record new information on mind maps at the end of each class period. Works with each group to help them develop their research questions. Asks students to use a T chart to record notes and reviews bibliographic citations. Shows students how to use *NoodleTools* to create their bibliography. Reviews the Drafting stage of the Writing Process.	Meets with students to help them develop a plan for conducting their research. Leads students in a discussion about possible information providers (outside the school), tools (search engines, databases, etc.), and resources they might use. Has developed a Favorites file of some Web sites about Native Americans. Tells students there will be a refresher session on using search engines for those who need an update. Helps students develop a list of keywords for searching based on their mind maps and research questions.	Meet in groups; make decisions about stereotyping source: books, magazines, pictures, film and video, etc. Groups develop research questions that focus both on stereotyping and accurate information about the lives of Native Americans. Develop a research plan for their group and begin to gather information. Record information on T charts and complete bibliographic citations. Make daily entries in their journals, reflecting on process.
9–11	Does individual coaching with student groups as they gather information. Reviews the Responding and Revising stage of the Writing Process.	Does individual coaching with student groups as they gather information. Coaches students to evaluate the information they are gathering (e.g., how to identify biased information).	Meet in their groups to share information and expand mind maps. Make daily entries in their journals, reflecting on process.

(Figure D.1 continues on page 138.)

Figure D.1 (*continues*)

12	Asks each student group to present their findings about stereotyping within a specific medium, using their mind maps. Following the presentations, asks students to identify the most common stereotypes that cross all of the media, such as biased language, omissions and inaccuracies about Native American life, etc. Asks students, "Now that you know the way stereotypes presented Native Americans, what information do you need to write a story, diary, or magazine article?"		Present findings represented on their mind maps about the stereotypes of Native Americans in their specific medium. Meet in small groups to decide on their product (story, diary, or magazine article). Depending on the writing product, some groups decide they need to do some additional research to be sure stories and diaries are historically accurate.
13–15	Works with students in groups, reviewing the writing practices for short story and diaries. Models using the information from a mind map to write a story. Shows students how a mind map can be changed to look like an outline using *Inspiration*.	Shows students how to use an *Inspiration* template, Language Arts-Comparison, as a format for comparing stereotypes that appeared in media to create an accurate portrayal of life for the American Indian.	Work on comparison charts to synthesize information. Work in the computer lab, writing their stories, diaries, or magazine article. Student mind maps on display in the LMC.
16–17	With LMS, assesses process and projects. Reviews the Proofreading and Publishing stages of the Writing Process.	Holds a discussion with students about the process they followed. Asks students to reflect on which strategies were the most important; which were frustrating; and what they might do differently next time. With teacher, assesses process and projects.	Share projects with other class members. Do peer evaluations based on historical accuracy. Review journals and write a reflection on overall process.

Note: The Writing Process is used with permission by the Davenport Community School District.

Collaboration Notes

The LMS and classroom teacher met several weeks before the unit begins with students to discuss strategies for integrating the Pathways model into the unit, teaching responsibilities, use of resources, etc.

The LMS and classroom teacher met shortly before the unit was to start to discuss final plan.

The LMS and classroom teacher met partway through the unit to consider progress, possible revisions, etc.

The LMS and classroom teacher met after the unit was completed to evaluate the unit

Resources

Note: All Web addresses accessed December 21, 2001.

Inspiration®. (1998–1999). (Ver. 6). Inspiration Software.

NoodleBib. (1999–2001). Debbie & Damon Abilock. [Online]. Available: http://www .noodletools.com/

Web Resources (Sites for a Favorites File)

The American West. (2001). [Online]. Available: http://www.theamericanwest.com/

The Basic Indian Stereotypes. (n.d.). Joseph Riverwind. [Online]. Available: http://www.bluecomcomics/stbasics.htm

Disney's Politically Correct Pocahontas. (1996). Jacquelyn Kilpatrick. Cineaste. [Online]. Available: http://www.lib.berkeley.edu/MRC/Pocahontas.html

The History Net. (2001). Primedia History Group. [Online]. Available: http://history .about.com/

Images of Indians of North America. (1999). Library of Congress. [Online]. Available: http://lcweb.loc.gov/rr/print/232_naov.html

Native Americans. (2001). [Online]. Available: http://www.sat.lib.tx.us/html/nativeam .htm

Native Americans: The Surprising Silents. (1996). Angela Aleiss. Cineaste. [Online]. Available: http://www.lib.berkeley.edu/MRC/NativeAmericans.html

NativeWeb. (1994–2001). [Online]. Available: http://www.nativeweb.org/ftsearch.php

The Only Good Indian Is a Dead Indian. (1995). Wolfgang Meider. De Proverbio. [Online]. Available: http://www.utas.edu.au/docs/flonta/DP,1,1,95/INDIAN.html

Themes: Native Americans. (1998–2001). Connecting Students. [Online]. Available: http://www.connectingstudents.com/themes/nat_amer.htm

Words and Deeds in American History. (1998). American Memory. Library of Congress. [Online]. Available: http://lcweb2.loc.gov/ammem/mcchtml/corhome.html

Fostering Systemic Change:

An Advance Organizer

Appendix E follows on pages 142–47.

Appendix E.1

Fostering Systemic Change
--- An Advance Organizer

Communicate
Cooperate
Question
Reflect
Evaluate
Refine
Trust

Page 1

Determine the Issue

Taking time to clearly identify the current situation and the desired change is vital to moving forward.

Why do we want or need to make this change?

What data or specific information indicates that a change needs to be made?

Identify Stakeholders

Involve others in brainstorming a list of positions/groups who would be interested in or affected by the change.

Who needs to be directly involved?

Who else would like to be involved?

Who or what groups will be impacted by the change?

Create a Core Team

The core team is critical to the success of the change effort. Choose wisely and be sure all stakeholders are represented. A core team member may represent more than one stakeholder group.

What groups need to be represented on the core team?

How big is too big?

© 2002 Pappas and Tepe

Appendix E.1

Fostering Systemic Change
--- An Advance Organizer

Page 2

Communicate
Cooperate
Question
Reflect
Evaluate
Refine
Trust

Gather Information

What is our plan for gathering information? Who are the experts and where will we find their research? Where might we see the desired change successfully in place? What do people who have gone through similar change have to say? How will we share our findings?

Pilot Some Possibilities

What type of pilot situations might we create to help field test ideas and suggestions? Can we identify 2-3? Who should be involved? What specifically are we looking for with these pilots? What is the timeline?

Reproducible from *Pathways to Knowledge®* and *Inquiry Learning* by Marjorie L. Pappas and Ann E. Tepe (Libraries Unlimited, 2002).

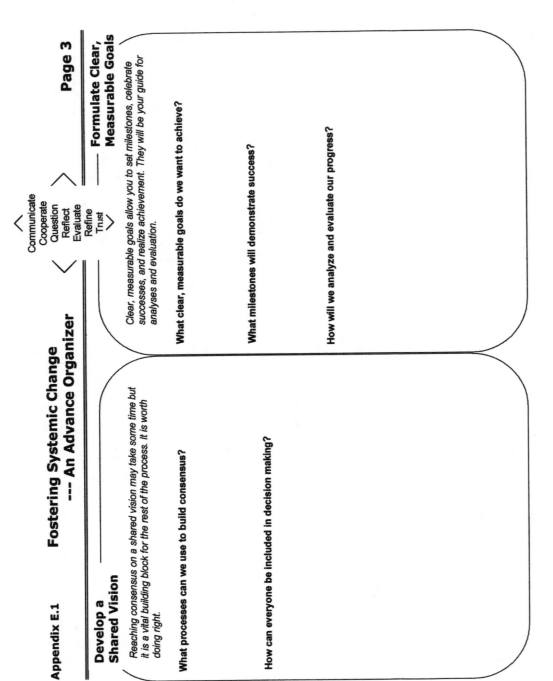

Appendix E.1

**Fostering Systemic Change
--- An Advance Organizer**

Page 3

Communicate
Cooperate
Question
Reflect
Evaluate
Refine
Trust

**Develop a
Shared Vision**

Reaching consensus on a shared vision may take some time but it is a vital building block for the rest of the process. It is worth doing right.

What processes can we use to build consensus?

How can everyone be included in decision making?

**Formulate Clear,
Measurable Goals**

Clear, measurable goals allow you to set milestones, celebrate successes, and realize achievement. They will be your guide for analyses and evaluation.

What clear, measurable goals do we want to achieve?

What milestones will demonstrate success?

How will we analyze and evaluate our progress?

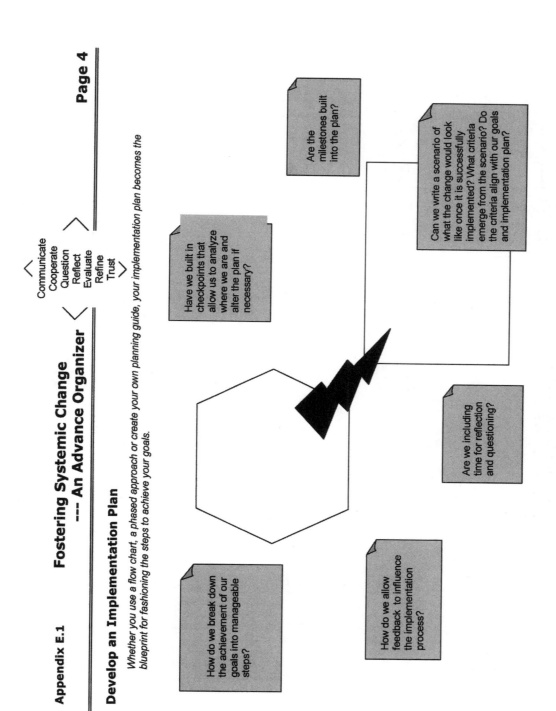

Appendix E.1 Fostering Systemic Change --- An Advance Organizer

Page 4

Communicate
Cooperate
Question
Reflect
Evaluate
Refine
Trust

Develop an Implementation Plan

Whether you use a flow chart, a phased approach or create your own planning guide, your implementation plan becomes the blueprint for fashioning the steps to achieve your goals.

Have we built in checkpoints that allow us to analyze where we are and alter the plan if necessary?

Are the milestones built into the plan?

Can we write a scenario of what the change would look like once it is successfully implemented? What criteria emerge from the scenario? Do the criteria align with our goals and implementation plan?

Are we including time for reflection and questioning?

How do we break down the achievement of our goals into manageable steps?

How do we allow feedback to influence the implementation process?

Appendix E.1

Fostering Systemic Change
--- An Advance Organizer

Page 5

Communicate
Cooperate
Question
Reflect
Evaluate
Refine
Trust

Provide Professional Development

What types of professional development are needed?

Are we equipped to design and deliver or do we need to bring in experts?

Facilitate Delivery

Who will be the participants and what preparation do they need?

What types of follow-up will we provide?

Analyze Results, Make Adjustments

How will we determine the success of the professional development?

How will we measure the long term impact on teaching and learning?

Based on the outcome of the professional development, do any changes need to be made to our Implementation Plan?

Providing the best possible professional development will greatly improve the success of the change effort.

Remember, additional professional development may be required.

© 2002 Pappas and Tepe

Reproducible from *Pathways to Knowledge*® *and Inquiry Learning* by Marjorie L. Pappas and Ann E. Tepe (Libraries Unlimited, 2002).

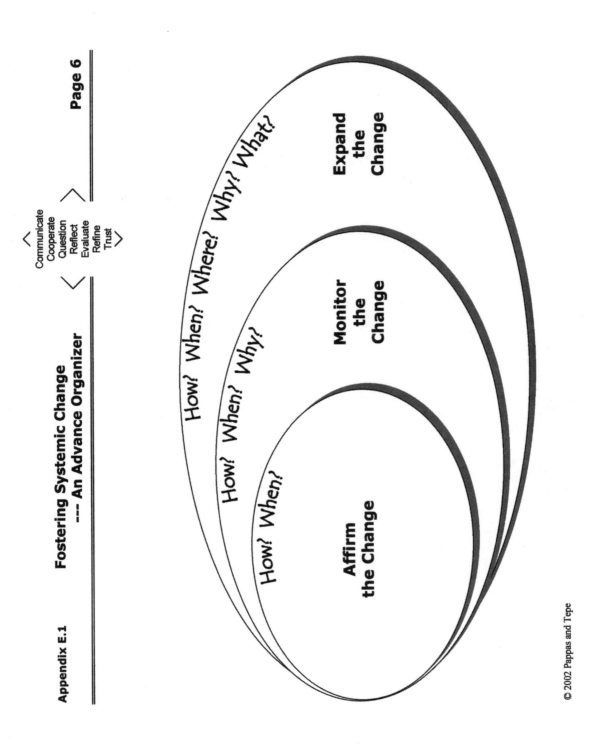

Appendix E.1

Fostering Systemic Change
--- An Advance Organizer

Page 6

Communicate
Cooperate
Question
Reflect
Evaluate
Refine
Trust

How? When? Where? Why? What?

How? When? Why?

How? When?

Expand
the
Change

Monitor
the
Change

Affirm
the Change

© 2002 Pappas and Tepe

Index

About the Authors

Marjorie Pappas teaches library science at Eastern Kentucky University. Prior to her university experience, Marjorie has been a children's librarian, a library media specialist, and a district supervisor of libraries and technology. She is the co-author of *Pathways to Knowledge*® with Ann Tepe; co-author of *Searching Electronic Resources* (Linworth, 1998); and a frequent writer for *School Library Activities Monthly*, focusing on information literacy, inquiry and authentic learning, and changing schooling for the information age.

Ann Tepe specializes in information literacy and technology integration for K–12 education and co-authored *Pathways to Knowledge*® with Marjorie Pappas. She teaches a web-enhanced course on information literacy and research for Wright State University in Ohio and is currently Director of Curriculum Development for Follett Software Company. Ann's background includes 25 years in education as a teacher and a library media director. She is a frequent presenter, workshop instructor, and editor. Ann can be reached at aetepe@concentric.net.